LIP-READING

PRINCIPLES AND PRACTISE

A HAND-BOOK FOR TEACHERS AND FOR SELF INSTRUCTION

BY

EDWARD B. NITCHIE, B. A.

PRINCIPAL OF THE NEW YORK SCHOOL FOR THE
HARD-OF-HEARING (INCORPORATED)

REVISED EDITION

A Digireads.com Book
Digireads.com Publishing
16212 Riggs Rd
Stilwell, KS, 66085

Lip-Reading
By Edward Nitchie
ISBN: 1-4209-2938-0

Please visit *www.digireads.com*

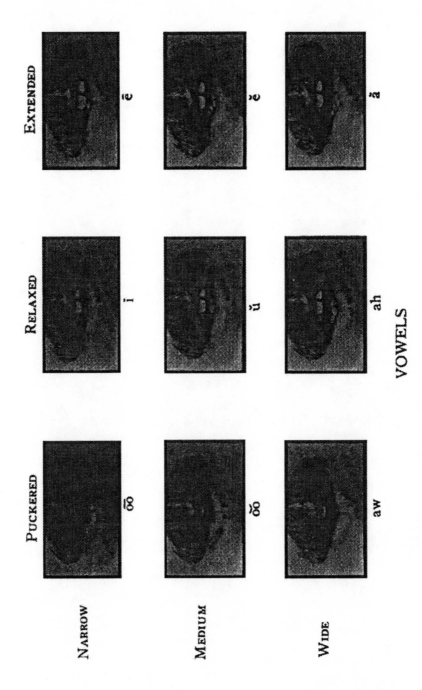

VOWELS

TO
MY TEACHERS

MUSIC

The ruder strains of music are denied,
The music of the human voice is lost,
The gulf of silence ever grows more wide,
My bark sails noiseless o'er life's swelling tide.
    By soundless billows tost.

But waves of harmony forever roll,
Orchestral cadences e'er fall and rise:
The mysteries of the part within God's whole,
The eternal whisperings of the Over-Soul
    Still 'trance me to the skies.

Ceaseless I hear the God of Nature call
Where green and gold chant anthems in the wood;
The meadows, daisy-capped, the silver ball
Of evening, stars and surging ocean—all.
    All sing of Love and Good.

It is the symphony of symphonies
Within my soul I hear,—to live, to work,
To turn my back on stumbling yesterdays,
Soul-sure defeats may e'en be victories
    If e'er I fight, nor shirk.

PREFACE

THIS book is the sixth of my text books on lip-reading, and as it embodies everything which the previous works contained, and considerable in addition, it is intended to replace them. Some parts of the book appeared originally as articles in *The Volta Review*, "a Monthly devoted to the problems of deafness," published in Washington, D. C., and acknowledgment of the courtesy of allowing reprinting is hereby made.

EDWARD B. NITCHIE

18 East 41st Street, NEW YORK.

PREFACE TO REVISED EDITION

WE have tried to put into the revision of this book all of the changes Mr. Nitchie had made in his methods prior to his death, but have not attempted to offer anything original. The work that is being done at the School was called forth and developed by Mr. Nitchie, and we are too near to his time to have any radical changes of real value to offer. Undoubtedly there will be further development in the years to come.

Both the system and methods embodied in this book are the results of years of study, and of experience in teaching. They were all carefully worked out, even to the smallest detail, and arranged in accordance with the newest psychological principles. In fact, the book has been pronounced "psychologically perfect."

We would call attention to the more important changes, such as the story program (pp. 54 and 96), the re-arrangement of the stories, and the new ones that have been added. Another change to be noted is the method of giving the Practise Words in Section III. (See p. 97.) Also the method of giving the Proverbs, and the review of the Colloquial Forms. The list of Homophenous Words has been revised.

MRS. EDWARD B. NITCHIE.

18 East 41st Street, NEW YORK.

CONTENTS

CONTENTS

APPENDICES

FOREWORD

LIP-READING is so presented in this work that it can be studied and mastered by the hard-of-hearing without the help of a teacher. The book is also intended for use, under a teacher's guidance, by the semi-mute, and by the congenitally deaf who have acquired speech and language. Even for the hard-of-hearing, personal instruction under an experienced teacher is, if possible, always advisable.

The book is divided into two parts: first, explanatory and directive, telling how to practise; second, giving materials and exercises, or telling what to practise. Anyone studying by himself, without experienced assistance, is advised to begin with Part I, Chapters IV–XI, doing only one thing at a time, as may be directed, for several practise periods until the different forms of practise are mastered. Then the work in Part II should be entered upon according to the outlines for study there given.

An experienced teacher, using the book, may begin directly with Part II, letting the pupil merely read the preliminary chapters.

PART I

CHAPTER I

IT is well known that the blind in a measure substitute hearing for sight; sounds of traffic in a busy street are a confused roar to the untrained ear, but to the experienced blind man they are a fairly reliable guide on his way.

Even to a greater degree can the deaf man train his eye to substitute for his deaf ears.

Watch the mouth of anyone who is speaking, and you will see many clearly defined movements of the lips, perhaps even of the tongue. The eye trained to associate certain movements with certain sounds has the power of interpreting these movements into words and sentences.

A very large percentage of the deaf are, I believe, incurable, at least at the present state of medical and surgical knowledge. The greatest loss to anyone who is deaf is the loss of understanding speech. Inability to hear music or the voices of nature is a deprivation; but inability to hear spoken language is a calamity, unless other means than the ear can be found to convey the message to the brain; for in the ability to understand spoken language lies the way not only to the pleasures of life, but to the truest necessities of the soul and body.

Deafness is a physical bar to employment second only to blindness, and bears especially heavily on the man who, dependent on others for his salary, becomes deaf in adult life. Lip-reading, or speech-reading, "that subtile art," as Dr. John Bulwer said in 1648, "which may inable one with an Observant Eie to Heare what any man Speaks by the moving of his Lips," is a valuable substitute for hearing, as far as spoken language is concerned, though, like any other substitutes, it has its limitations. By it the sense of sight is forced to interpret a medium for expressing thought which, throughout the history of the race, has been developed for the needs of the sense of hearing. I shall show later how imperfectly spoken language is fitted to the requirements of successful lip-reading.

The problem of the teacher varies according to the class of the deaf to which his pupil belongs, for the deaf-mute's needs are only in part the needs of the hard-of-hearing. My work lies with the hard-of-hearing—and by that term I mean those who, either partly or totally deaf, became so after having acquired speech and language—and it is of their problem of which I shall speak particularly. It is not only their problem; its solution becomes also the solution of the problem of the deaf-mute *after* he acquires speech and language.

The problem of teaching lip-reading is truly a psychological problem. Both the eyes and the mind must be trained, but mind-training is the more important factor.

The difficulties for the eyes to overcome are two: first, the obscurity of many of the movements, and second, the rapidity of their formation. That spoken language is not well adapted to the purpose of lip-reading is evident from the many sounds that are formed within the mouth or even in the throat. The difference between vocal and non-vocal consonants is invisible to the eye. The aspirate *h*, as in "hat," cannot be seen; there is no visible difference between "hat" and "at." The consonants formed by the back of the tongue and soft palate, *k*, hard *g*, *ng*, are seldom revealed to the eye of the lip-reader; likewise, certain tongue consonants, as *t, d, n,* and *y,* present almost insuperable difficulties. Double tongue consonants, as *nt, nd, lt, ld,* are also just as indefinite and obscure in their visible formation.

Rapidity of the movements is another serious difficulty in the way of successful lip-reading. From one-twelfth to one-thirteenth of a second is the average time per movement in ordinary speech. This is the average, but some movements are of course slower, while others, particularly those for unaccented syllables, are much quicker.

With such difficulties as these, the wonder is that anyone can read the lips at all. Eye-training can never eliminate them, though it can lessen them in a measure. The method should aim first always to study or see the movements in words or sentences, not formed singly by themselves. Sounds pronounced singly all tend to be exaggerated, and many of them even to be grossly mispronounced. Moreover, one movement often modifies decidedly the appearance of another connected with it in a word. For example, long *e* usually tends to show a slight drawing back of the corners of the mouth, as in "thief;" but,

after *sh*, as in "sheep," this is scarcely
visible.

In the second place the method should aim
always to study or see the movements as the
words are pronounced quickly. It is true that
it would be easier to see them when spoken
slowly, but it is also true that to produce the
best results the eye should be trained from
the first to see things as they must always be
seen in ordinary speech, and that is rapidly.

And, in the third place, the method should
aim to inculcate a nearly infallible accuracy
and quickness of perception of the easier
movements, leaving to the mind in large
measure the task of supplying the harder
movements.

With the eye thus trained it often happens
that the lip-reader's impression is that of
actually hearing what is said. If I put the
tubes of a phonograph into my ears, so that
I can hear every word, and close my eyes,
unbidden and without conscious effort the
vision of the moving lips of the speaker forming the flow of the words passes before my
mind.

Although it is not possible for the eye to
see each and every movement, it is possible

for the mind to grasp a complete impression without even the consciousness that it has "supplied" so many of the movements and sounds. The chief difficulties in the way of the mind in lip-reading may be indicated by describing that type of mind which is uniformly most successful, and that is a mind which is quick to respond to impressions, or quick in its reaction time, and a mind in which the synthetic qualities are dominant. The difficulties, then, are to overcome the opposite conditions or tendencies, and the aim is to develop the mind to the utmost along the line of these favoring conditions.

Fortunately thought is quicker than speech. Testing myself with a selected passage that I know by heart it takes me fifteen seconds to think of it word by word, and thirty-five seconds to read it aloud. To develop quick perception, *practise* is the essential; that is, slow speech, word-by-word utterance, must be avoided, and all forms of exercise must be given to the pupil up to the limit of speed which his ability will allow. This undoubtedly makes the work harder for the time being, but it results in more rapid progress.

Not only is thought quicker than speech:

thought need not formulate every word to have clear conceptions. Thought skips; thought looks ahead and anticipates. So that a correct understanding of an idea is possible without a word-for-word accuracy. That is the way the baby understands what is said to him. I would say to my little boy, when a year and a half old, "How does daddy shave himself in the morning?" That he understood every word was not possible; probably "daddy" and "shave" were the only ones he really knew. But that he understood what I said he made evident when he went through the motion of shaving his own face with his finger.

The method of mind-training should aim to develop this power of grasping thoughts as wholes, and to avoid strictly anything that will enhance the opposite tendency of demanding verbal accuracy before anything is understood at all. Minds of the latter type are literal, analytical, unimaginative. Yet there are very few who are altogether of this kind; most of us, however analytical, have some synthetic powers, some ability of putting things together, of constructing the whole from the parts, of quick intuition. It is by developing these powers that real success in lip-reading can be attained, and it is by working along these lines that the surest way is found in the end to the understanding of every word. Even those who hear, often have an experience like this: Some one will make a remark which you fail to understand; the word "what" is on your lips, but before it is fairly uttered the whole sentence will come to you like a flash. When this intuitive, synthetic power is highly developed, the "natural-born" lip-reader is the result.

I feel sure, from what is known of the men, that Prescott, the historian, would have easily learned lip-reading, while the analytical Bancroft would have found it much more difficult; that Seton Thompson would be quick to master it, and that John Burroughs would be slower; that Roosevelt would be an expert, and that Hughes would be a novice. I have repeatedly found among my pupils that those who can play music readily at sight are apt in reading the lips, for such ability implies quick reaction time and the intuitive mind.

What degree of skill can a lip-reader expect to attain? How long does it take? These are natural questions, but cannot be answered

categorically. What some can attain in three
months, others cannot acquire short of a year;
and the highest degree of skill, as in any art,
is open only to the few. But three lessons a
week for three months will, with most pupils,
give a very satisfactory and practical skill.
I may be pardoned if I speak of myself. I
can sometimes understand a lecture or sermon, depending upon conditions of light,
etc.; less often can I understand a play. I am
called a good lip-reader, but I know better
ones. With a very few exceptions, such a
degree of skill is possible to every one as to
make home life and social friendships a joy
once more, and, though it may not be an
infallible resource in business, it may for all
be an invaluable aid. Lip-reading can never
do all that good ears ought to do, but what it
can do is almost a miracle.

Two objections to lip-reading I occasionally
hear: (1) That it is too great a strain on the
eyes, and (2) that, by relieving the ears from
hearing, there is a tendency to deterioration
in hearing from lack of exercise.

The strain upon the eyes at first is truly
no small one; but I have repeatedly found
that those who complain of eye-strain during

their first lessons, later never think any more about it. I have not strong eyes, and now, though I use them in reading the lips every day and all day long, they are seldom overtired. If the lip-reader is careful from the first to cease using the eyes at the first symptom of tire, I believe that no harm can result and gradually the eyes will be able to do more and more.

The objection in regard to the deterioration of hearing I believe to be the reverse of true. Dr. Albert Barnes, in "The Dietetic and Hygienic Gazette," of October, 1909, said: "People with ear-strain should spare the hearing as much as possible, and, instead of straining the ear to catch what is said, they should watch the lips more. In other words, the eyes should be called upon to help the ears." Moreover, with pupils who have enough hearing to hear the sound of the voice, I advise and encourage them to use ears and eyes in fullest coöperation, one helping the other.

Under such circumstances, and also in view of the fact that the ear involuntarily gets exercise with every sound that comes to it, whether the strain to hear is made or not, I do not see how any harm can be done to the ears by lip-reading, and in all my experience I have never found any evidence of such harm. On the contrary, several times pupils have reported to me an actual betterment of the hearing, though how much lip-reading had to do with it and how much other conditions I do not pretend to say.

Lip-reading, then, is not a cure for deafness, nor is it even a cure for all the ills of deafness; but from some of the worst ills it is a true alleviation. It takes first place on the majority of occasions over all mechanical devices. For those completely deaf, or so deaf as to make mechanical devices out of the question, lip-reading is the only resource. For those whose deafness still allows them to hear the sound of the voice, it obviates the necessity of using these more or less cumbersome and inconvenient contrivances. Even at such times when these devices can be used to advantage, watching the lips helps to make them more useful and more reliable. Under any circumstances, lip-reading has in it the power to make deafness of whatever degree much easier to bear.

CHAPTER II

THE preceding chapter, *The Eye as a Substitute for Deaf Ears*, tells the underlying basis for success in lip-reading. The teacher should know how to develop the requisite qualities in each pupil to the utmost. Every one has three sides, the physical, the mental, the spiritual. It is a truism that perfect development exists only when the development of each side is symmetrical. It is so in lip-reading. The eyes (physical), the mind, and even the soul qualities, must all have proper attention to attain the highest success possible in each individual case.

The eyes must be trained (1) to be accurate, (2) to be quick, (3) to retain visual impressions, and (4) to do their work subconsciously.

The first of these requisites is so obvious that there is perhaps a tendency to over-emphasize it in the neglect of the others. Of course the eyes cannot be too accurate; the

14

danger is in training for accuracy alone regardless of other needs. To secure accuracy in lip-reading, the pupil must know exactly what to look for. The careful description of each movement tells him this; and the teacher should also show it to him on the mouth. The *movement words* (see Part II, Section III, under the description of each movement), in which each new movement is developed in contrast and in connection with previously studied movements, provide the best possible material for training in accuracy. The *contrast words* also, by showing the differences between similar movements, direct the eyes to an accurate study of the decisive characteristics. And the *practise words*, giving each new movement in combination with all the fundamental movements, both before and after, show how the movements are mutually modified by association. Directions for using this material are given in their proper place.

Accuracy alone is not sufficient. The quickness of natural speech makes it imperative that the eyes be trained to be quick. For this reason, from the very first, all forms of exercise of whatever kind should be practised always as rapidly as the ability of the pupil will allow. Particularly all review work should be rapid. It will be easier for the pupil to have the teacher enunciate slowly, but the rapid enunciation, up to the limit of the pupil's ability, will do him considerably more good.

The importance of training the visual memory is clear from the fact that often the lip-reader will get the first part of a sentence from the last; that is, the understanding of a few words toward the end of a sentence, aided by the memory of preceding facial movements, will enable the lip-reader to construct the whole. Sentence practise is always good for developing this power; but at no time should the pupil be allowed to interrupt the teacher until either a whole sentence, or at least a clause, has been completed. Other practise for developing the power of visual memory will be found directed under the vowel and consonant exercises (see p. 253) where the pupil is required to carry three, four, or even five unrelated words in mind and to repeat them in order.

All this work for the eyes is in its essence analytic. The conscious work of the mind in lip-reading, however, must be synthetic.

Hence the eyes must be trained to do their work subconsciously. To do so, the eyes must work by habit, and to form these habits much repetition in practise is necessary. To give an exercise once may train for accuracy, but not for subconscious accuracy. It is absolutely essential, therefore, that the pupil and the teacher should go over and over and over things until they are truly mastered.

The essentials in training the mind are to develop (1) synthetic ability, (2) intuition, (3) quickness, and (4) alertness.

The necessity of synthetic ability has been sufficiently explained in Chapter I. The work directed in Chapter V, *How to Use Stories,* is all intended to develop synthesis, and the question practise as there directed is especially helpful. Every kind of sentence practise is an aid, including the work directed under that heading, Chapter X, and the Colloquial Forms (p. 282) and the Homophenous Words (p. 301.)

Closely allied with the synthetic quality is intuition. The lip-reader who has the power of intuitively jumping to the right conclusions has a potent aid to synthesis. Good development practise for the intuitive powers, leading the mind to look for natural sequences of thought, is to be found in the use of stories by telling them in different words (see Chapter V), in the use of words as a basis for sentences built around the thought suggested by them (see Chapter IX), in the use of sentences to develop other sentences associated with them in idea (see Chapter X), and in conversation and in more formal talks along some chosen theme (see Chapter IV).

It is just as important for the mind to be quick as for the eyes. It sometimes happens that the eye will see quickly but the mind will interpret slowly. To develop quickness of mind the teacher should insist upon a quick response in all work where the pupil is required to repeat what has been said.

By alertness I do not mean the same as quickness, but rather an openness of the mind to impressions and a readiness for new turns of thought. It is not uncommon to find a pupil who clings to false impressions, loth to cast them aside, even when told they are wrong. Such a pupil should have his attention directed to his failing and be cautioned to guard against it at all times. The skipping practise directed for the stories (Chapter V) and the skipping practice directed for words

(Chapter IX) and sentences (Chapter X) will all help to develop mental alertness.

In my wide experience with the deaf and hard-of-hearing it has seemed that the thing most needed by them is access to the spiritual springs of human life. No other class of people is so shut off from these springs, for they are to be found above all else in the mutual intercourse of soul with soul. By the fact of their deafness, such human companionship is denied in very large measure. The deaf are thrown upon themselves and their own thoughts and resources. As they have expressed it to me again and again, they are "hungry" for a real conversation; they are "lonely," though surrounded by family and friends. It is not surprising that morbidness, hopelessness and the "blues," and lack of courage and self-confidence mark their increasing deafness and consequent increasing isolation.

The difficulties of the teacher with a pupil like that are truly of a spiritual nature. It is a hopeless task to try to make a successful lip-reader of one whose "Oh! I can't" attitude stands in the way of every achievement, unless that spirit of despair be supplanted by the

spirit of "I can" and "I will." It is true
that increasing skill in lip-reading tends to
dispel these morbid conditions of mind, but
it is also true that these morbid conditions
stand squarely in the way of such increasing
skill. The mere study of lip-reading *per se*
cannot be relied upon to banish the "blues"
and lack of self-confidence and courage. So it
becomes of utmost importance for the teacher
to work directly upon these spiritual conditions. Not obviously of course, still less by
nagging; nor yet by pity, nor even by sympathy of the wrong kind, (though sympathy
of the right kind is a powerful agent).

I can lay down rules for the training of the
eye in lip-reading and rules, though more
elastic ones, for training the mind. But rules
for developing these desired spiritual qualities
cannot so well be formulated. I think, however, I can make some suggestions which will
help guide the teacher along the road.

Of course no two pupils are alike in their
spiritual qualities or spiritual needs. They
are not all as "blue" as he whose needs I
have been picturing. But I suppose there
is no one who cannot stand a helping hand
along the road to cheer and courage.

It is axiomatic that to impart spiritual qualities you must have them. That is why I regard "personality" as the most valued asset of the teacher. A strong personality and the power to make that personality felt as an influence toward the best things are fundamental qualities of the great teacher in any subject, and they apply with special force to the teacher of lip-reading.

Sympathy of the right kind is strongly needed: not the kind that turns the pupil's thoughts more than ever on his affliction, for that strengthens his habit of self-pity; but the kind that, while acknowledging the affliction, gives the pupil a metaphorical slap on the back, stirs him to stand by his own efforts and work out his own salvation. Many pupils rely on the teacher to do all the work, make all the effort. To say nothing of their lack of effort, their very attitude is an insuperable bar to achievement. Win over such a pupil to work with you and half the battle is won.

Meet every mood of discouragement with cheer and hope. Don't be sparing of praise for good work well done. Don't be impatient with failure, especially if the effort be true. Hold up the bright side of the picture always.

Encourage by example of what others have achieved. These are some of the essentials in the teacher's spiritual attitude toward the pupil.

Be the friend of your pupil, not merely his teacher. Take an interest in the things that interest him, and gain his interest, too, in the things that lie close to your own heart. Friendship opens many a door to helpfulness that otherwise would remain closed. Be his friend, but don't forget that you are his teacher too. Don't let friendship make you "easy with the pupil," nor cause you to let down the bars to indolence and weaken the spur to faithful effort. Expect, and let your whole attitude demand, the pupil's best.

The teacher who works in this spirit with his pupils will have the joy not only of seeing them advance more quickly in the art of lip-reading, but also and especially of seeing them live happier, cheerier, braver, and more useful lives.

CHAPTER III

IT is not easy to be deaf; it is a mighty hard thing; and it is often made harder for us by the unnecessary friction between us and our friends arising from the fact of our deafness. That is why I ask you, the friends of the deaf, to consider some of the ways and means by which you can help to make our lot easier for us. I do not mean to scold or find fault, but to help—to help you to help us. If at times I speak plainly, even bluntly, I trust you will pardon it in view of my purpose.

If it is a question of blame, we ourselves must assume our share of it. It is often our attitude that makes things hard for both you and us. For one thing, we are prone to be too sensitive. And yet that is the most natural thing in the world. I suppose every man or woman who carries a physical affliction is more or less sensitive. The lame man, the blind man, the humpback, the stammerer,

23

all have a fellow feeling in this regard. But the peculiarity of deafness is that it has the unhappy faculty of drawing down ridicule upon its victim.

If a lame man stumbles and falls, nobody laughs; everybody rushes to help him to his feet. If a blind man runs into a stone wall, every one is all sympathy. But let a deaf man make a mistake, due to his deafness, and everybody laughs. Yes, I know they do not laugh at him; they laugh at his mistake. If it were only easy for him to realize that, it would save him intense mortification. I suppose there is not one of us who has not felt at some time or other that he wished the floor would open and swallow him up.

When I was at college, one of the members of the glee club was very bald; but he wore a wig. At the concerts he sang a solo:

> "I'd rather have fingers than toes,
> I'd rather have eyes than a nose;
> And as for my hair,
> I'm so glad it's all there,
> I'll be sore as can be when it goes."

And with the last word he would snatch the wig from his head. Of course everybody laughed; but the point is, that *he laughed with them*. If we who are deaf would cultivate the saving grace of laughing at our mistakes, it would take all the sting out of them.

On the other hand, there is the danger that those who laugh at us may get the worst of it themselves. John Wanamaker tells the story of a deaf man named Brown, who was disposed to stinginess.

"He never married, but he was very fond of society, so one day he felt compelled to give a banquet to the many ladies and gentlemen whose guest he had been.

"They were amazed that his purse-strings had been unloosed so far, and they thought he deserved encouragement; so it was arranged that he should be toasted. One of the most daring young men of the company was selected, for it took a lot of nerve to frame and propose a toast to so unpopular a man as Miser Brown. But the young man rose. And this is what was heard by every one except Brown, who never heard anything that was not roared into his ear:

"'Here's to you, Miser Brown. You are no better than a tramp, and it is suspected that you got most of your money dishonestly.

We trust that you may get your just deserts yet, and land in the penitentiary.'

"Visible evidences of applause made Brown smile with gratification. He got upon his feet, raised his glass to his lips, and said, 'The same to you, sir.'"

Inattention is one of our chief faults. Not hearing what is going on around us, we are apt to withdraw into our own thoughts; and then, when some one does speak to us, we are far away. We need to be more on the alert than others, just because we cannot hear; our quickness of eye must make up for our aural slowness. To you, our friends, I wish to make the suggestion that you draw our attention, not by touching us, not by a violent waving of the arm or perhaps the handkerchief, not by shouting to us, but by a quiet movement of the hand within our range of vision. We are sensitive. Anything that brings our affliction into the limelight of the observation of others cuts like a lash; and there are few things we dislike more than having our attention attracted by a poke or a pull, though a gentle touch is sometimes not disagreeable.

Another of our faults is a tendency to seclusiveness. We not only draw into our own thoughts when others are present; we often retire from company into the solitude of a book or magazine, or avoid company altogether. It is a rudeness, I know, to pick up a book and read when in the company of others; yet it is a rudeness that even our friends ought sympathetically to condone. And, moreover, I ask you which is the greater rudeness, that of our taking up our book or that of your passing around the sweets of conversation and offering none to us? Truly, we ought not to seclude ourselves, but we need your help.

We have our faults, and so have you, and your chief fault, as far as we are concerned, is that you do not realize what it means to be deaf. Occasionally I hear some one say he wishes he might be deaf for a little while; he would be glad if some of the disturbing noises might be eliminated. Oh, deafness is not so bad, he opines; it has its advantages— which I do not deny; but they are not the advantages he has in mind. I sometimes wish that such a person might truly be deaf for say a year without the knowledge that at the end of that time his hearing would be restored to him. Then he would find the one-time disturbing noises had become music in his ears, and that the advantages of deafness, provided he had met his affliction in the right spirit, were of a spiritual and not of a physical nature.

It is thoughtlessness, due to ignorance of conditions, that is the cause of most of the troubles between you and us. It is not selfishness—not usually, at any rate—but just that you do not stop to think. And that is why I am writing to you: to help you to understand and show the same thoughtfulness toward us as you instinctively would show toward the blind.

There is one book that every friend of the deaf ought to read, "Deafness and Cheerfulness," by the Rev. A. W. Jackson. Intended for the deaf themselves, it has a still greater value, I believe, for their friends. The little brochure, "The Deaf in Art and the Art of Being Deaf," by Grace Ellery Channing, is also good. Such reading will help you to put yourselves in our place.

It is easy enough for us to imagine what lameness and what blindness mean; probably most of us have been more or less lame at some time or other, and we are all of us blind when in the dark. But it is a much more difficult thing for the hearing to imagine the full calamity of deafness. Think how much of the sweetness of life comes to you through your ears. The joys of companionship and fellowship with other men and women are dependent on our understanding what they have to say. Try for one week to imagine what it would be like if every spoken word that comes to you were lost. Think each time, "Suppose I had not heard that," and when you have finally comprehended what the world of silence is, your sympathetic understanding will go a long way toward lightening our cross.

If you could really put yourselves in our place, one of the first things you would realize is that there are few things that so irritate as to have you shout at us. It is so unnecessary and uncalled for, and makes us the center of unenvied observation. We will in fact understand you better if instead of shouting you enunciate clearly and distinctly and make your voice as vibrant as may be possible.

In a general conversation we greatly need your help. A certain deaf man expressed the unuttered view of many another when he said, "I enjoy a conversation with one person, but when a third breaks in upon us, h—— enters the room with him." In nine cases out of ten the deaf man is given no share in general conversation, and for all purposes of social enjoyment he might almost as well be marooned on a desert island.

General conversation is hard for us to understand, even though we be skillful readers of the lips. As we all know, it is very much easier to follow conversation when we know the subject. When two people are talking we may say that each has a one-half share; when three, each has a one-third share, and so on. This is true provided all can hear. But if one is deaf, while it is still true he has a half-share when only two are talking, when three are talking he has no share at all! If only the others would talk to him! But no, they talk to each other, and he is out of it. My advice to you, then, in a general conversation, is: "Talk to us." The others will hear you, and it will give us the benefit of sharing in the conversation, of knowing the subject, and of greatly increased ease of understanding.

There are times, I know, when it is not

possible to talk to us, or others may be talking who have not the thoughtfulness to do so. Then what we ask of you is not to rehash the conversation after the topic has been talked out, but by a word or two at the beginning to indicate to us the subject.

The suggestions I have given you so far will apply whether we are lip-readers or not. Now I wish to give you some suggestions that will help us in our endeavor to hear with the eyes. For one thing, let the light be on your face, not on ours. It requires only a little thoughtfulness to see to this important requisite. In my own family such thoughtfulness has become so instinctive as to be a habit, and the endeavor to get the light right is always a first thought when any of the family are talking to me.

The exaggeration of the facial movements, "mouthing," usually arises on your part from the best intentions to help us understand. You mean well, but as a matter of fact you are making it harder for us. Such exaggeration throws the mouth out of all natural movement and formation, and makes it impossible for us to know just what we do see. All we ask of you is that you speak distinctly, and then the movements of your lips and tongue will take care of themselves.

Closely associated with your endeavor to help us by exaggeration is the endeavor to help through a word-by-word manner of talking. The human mind naturally takes in the thought as a whole and not piecemeal, one word at a time. It is exasperation to ask us to understand in that way. How much of the thought of this printed page would you get if you stopped to think about each word separately? Like the man who could not see the woods for the trees, so when—you—talk—this—way we cannot see the thought for the words. If it is necessary to speak slowly to us, let it be smoothly, connectedly, and not word by word.

Another of your well-meant efforts to help us consists in repeating for us a single word that we have failed to understand; it is much easier for us to get the word in its thought connection in a sentence. For the same reason, the long phrase is usually easier than the short phrase; as, for example, "Will you get me a drink of water?" presents much less difficulty than "Will you get me a drink?"

In your choice of words, try to choose if possible those that have the most movement of the lips. If you want to say "a quarter," choose the words "twenty-five cents." For "fifty cents," however, you should say "half a dollar," for not only does the latter phrase have more lip-movement, but it is also true that "fifty cents" might easily be mistaken for "fifteen cents." As another example, notice as you say the sentences how much plainer and more pronounced the lip-movements are for "What beautiful weather we are having" than for "Isn't it a nice day?"

Proper names are always hard, because we have as a rule no context to help us. When you introduce us to strangers, be careful to speak the name clearly and distinctly direct to us. Not infrequently I find my hearing friends introducing me with a decided emphasis on my own name, as though it were very necessary that I should understand that, and with the name of my new acquaintance so mumbled that I do not know whether he is Teufelsdröckh or Smith. Again, when in conversation you are referring to some one by name, a short explanatory phrase will often help us wonderfully; as, "I like to deal at Scudder and Singer's—*the meat market, you know.*"

I have presented to you some of our problems, believing that you can help us. Yet I realize that you cannot do it all—that we must coöperate. And the first thing for us to do in the way of self-help is frankly to acknowledge our deafness. I think no greater mistake can be made from the standpoint of our own comfort and peace of mind than that of trying to conceal the fact that we cannot hear. It is not only sensitiveness, it is also a feeling of shame, as though we had done some wrong, that impels us to try to hide our failing ears. We need the advice of the lunatic in the story. All day long a fisherman had been sitting on the bank of the stream and had not caught a thing. All day long the lunatic had watched him from a window in the neighboring insane asylum. At last the man in the window could endure it no longer, and he shouted to the fisherman: "Hey, there, you poor fool! Come on inside!"

So we need to come on inside the ranks to which we belong, frankly, realizing that it is no crime to be deaf, and then try by every means in our power to make our lives normal and sane. That is what we are striving to do, and we ask your help that our burden of deafness may be lightened as much as possible.

CHAPTER IV

CONVERSATION PRACTISE

THE end and aim of all lip-reading practise is facility in understanding conversation. But to this end conversation practise alone is not enough. It is common to hear a pupil say: "I have practise in talking with people all the time; I don't need any other practise." If you were studying music on the piano, would it be sufficient only to play pieces, and never scales, chords, and exercises? If you were studying French, would it be sufficient only to converse, and to know nothing of forms, idiom, and grammar?

Skill in reading the lips certainly can be gained by conversation practise alone, but neither so speedily nor so thoroughly as when such conversation practise is supplemented by the practise of exercises of the various kinds that have been explained in my previous papers. Conversely it is true that the practise of those exercises alone will not sufficiently avail unless they are put to practical application in what is the end of them all, conversation.

In conversation, however, the conscious effort of the lip-reader should be not to think of or to try to see the forms, movements, syllables, etc., but simply to grasp the thought of the speaker. The perception of the movements must be left to take care of itself; you should know them, but not think of them; your recognition of them should be subconscious. When you read the printed page, you do not think of the individual letters, yet, without being conscious of it, you see them. When you play the piano, the printed notes are your guide, but (if you are truly skillful) those notes are transformed into music through your fingers without your stopping to think what the notes are. The successful student of a foreign language uses the language like a native without a thought of form, case, tense, construction and the other demands of grammar. In each instance the technical knowledge is there, and is used, but it has been relegated to the lower centers of the brain that do things by habit without requiring attention or direction.

It should be the same in lip-reading, for the mind has not the time nor the power to think of the elements and to construct the idea therefrom, to conduct consciously a process of analysis and synthesis, at the same time. In all conversation practise therefore let the elements take care of themselves and focus your effort on the endeavor to grasp the thought.

There are more ways than one of securing conversation practise. The beginning should be in forming the habit of always watching the mouth, not the eyes, of a speaker. For some the formation of this habit is difficult, but it must be formed if success is to be attained—it is one of the essentials. Even though you hear the sound of the voice, even though you actually hear every word, watch the mouth too. The eyes are expressive, and with many people so is the whole face. But no part of the face reveals so much as the moving lips and tongue. Moreover, though your gaze is focused on the mouth, all the rest of the face is visible to you. The most skillful lip-reader would find his difficulties doubled if he could see only the mouth and the rest of the face were masked; but if he could see the rest of the face and not the mouth, the difficulties would be increased a hundred-fold.

Always watching the mouth means more than watching only when you are personally addressed. It means watching it in general conversation, watching it in public places, watching it in the case of a preacher or lecturer, in short, *always* watching it. If you are very deaf and still with little skill in reading the lips, you will probably understand only words here and there, and stray sentences, unless the conversation is turned directly to you. But every little counts and is a step toward more. If only slightly deaf, and if you hear the sound of the voice more or less, you should find real help in this habit, even from the first; for your eyes will be coöperating with your ears, one helping the other, and much that either would lose alone will be understood.

More definite practise can be obtained when you and some one friend are talking together. If your friend is like many others, he will persist in talking loud, a habit formed before the days of your endeavor to read the lips. Don't let him. Over and over again, probably, you will have to tell him "not to

talk so loud;" he forgets. But continue to
tell him until the new habit is formed of talking to you more softly,—not in a whisper,
I do not mean that, nor even in a low tone,
but naturally, or so that you hear something,
enough with the help of your eyes to understand, but not enough to understand without
such help. Such a habit will mean for him
greatly increased ease of conversing with
you, increased delight in such conversation
for both of you, and good lip-reading practise
for yourself.

When talking with two or more friends, the
responsibility on your part to help yourself
is a serious one. In a previous chapter I
have said: "It is very much easier to follow
conversation when we know the subject.
When two people are talking we may say
that each has a one-half share; when three,
each has a one-third share, and so on. This
is true provided all can hear. But if one
is deaf, while it is still true he has a half share
when only two are talking, when three are
talking he has no share at all! If only the
others would talk to him! But no, they talk
to each other, and he is out of it."

It is not an easy task for us to "butt in" and

divert that one-third share to us, where it belongs; we need and ought to have help from
the others. But it is fundamentally *our* task,
and by performing it as we should we gain
practise, and pleasure, and a great victory.

All these ways of securing practise in conversation are casual, yet not for that reason to
be despised. They should not, however, be
allowed to usurp the place of definite conversation practise, practise in which you do not
hear a sound. In this case, if you are only
slightly deaf, it will be necessary for your
friend or assistant to talk very, very softly—a
low voice is better than a whisper—and for
you not to sit too close, and, perhaps, to put a
bit of cotton in your ears. Choose themes
for your conversation in which you are mutually interested, and then let it take its course.
Only you must remember that conversation
implies give and take; you must do your
share, and not expect a monologue from your
assistant.

Some bits of advice for your general intercourse with people will be useful. Do not get
into the habit of demanding that you understand every word. Try to cultivate the power
of grasping the thought, of constructing the

sentence from one or more key words. Let the speaker continue talking until you catch the idea, and do not interrupt unless you feel that what is being said is something you ought to know about. In a general conversation, much can be lost (so to speak) without losing much. Try to follow the sense of what is said, rather than to "dig out" each word. If you lose a word, do not stop to think what the word was, for as surely as you do, you will lose all that follows. What is lost, is lost; never mind it; but continue to try to follow the thought. So long as you do follow the thought successfully, do not interrupt. You should, of course, interrupt if you lose the thought completely. Though it does not pay, as a rule, if we lose a word here and there, to interrupt the speaker, we must be very careful not to carry "bluffing" too far. To pretend to understand, when really scarcely anything is understood, is inexcusable.

The necessity of a good light on the speaker's face should be realized. A light that makes visible the action of the tongue is a great help. A light from above, such as a high gas-light, will not do this; the light should be as nearly as possible on a level with the face. If you find the speaker's face is in the shadow, either change your own position to a more favorable one, or ask the speaker to change his.

Rapid and indistinct utterance will be the root of much of your trouble. If you can persuade your friends to speak more distinctly, and to address the conversation directly to you, it will be a great help, but they must be cautioned to speak naturally, and not to "mouth," or exaggerate, as this will only increase your lip-reading difficulties.

Necessity has been called the mother of invention. It is also the mother of achievement. The achievements of all lip-readers will be surer and more rapid, the more they force upon themselves the necessity of understanding with the eyes. We can best lay this necessity upon ourselves at first in our home life. As far as may be possible, communication with members of the family should be by sight. Requests for different articles at the table may quickly be learned and understood in this way. And at all other times the endeavor should be made not to depend upon the ears when the eyes can serve.

CHAPTER V

To know how to use stories and reading-books for practise, we must know why we use them. There is such a thing as practising in the wrong way. In spite of the opinion held by some that "just practise" is all that is necessary, it is not so much the amount of practise as it is the kind of practise that produces the best results. There are right ways and wrong ways of doing everything, and in lip-reading it is possible to practise in such a way as incidentally to do absolute harm. One hour of the right kind of practise is worth five hours of the wrong kind.

Keep in mind that the aim of all practise is to acquire skill in understanding *conversation*. In ordinary conversation people talk rapidly. No lip-reader, however skillful, can be absolutely sure of seeing every word. But he can be sure of understanding all the thought, even though words be lost.

44

The best lip-readers are invariably those who have the power of grasping the thought as a whole, and not through a word-by-word deciphering of the sentence. And in the end, the surest way of understanding practically every word, is not through the word-by-word method, but is through developing this synthetic power of constructing the whole from the parts. That is, if the whole thought is understood, the visual memory of the rest of the sentence will most surely, and usually subconsciously, supply the missing words.

The chief value of stories and reading matter as material for lip-reading practise lies in their use toward developing the synthetic qualities mentioned; to develop the right habits of mind—the mental attitude that is quickest to understand conversation—stories are invaluable.

There are stories *and* stories. Fundamentally the style should be as near the colloquial as possible, the style in which people talk rather than in which they write. For this is the style that gives us the natural sequences of thought, the natural associations of ideas. It is not simply that the story should have a good deal of conversation in it, but that throughout the sentences should be simple, not involved, and the sequence of thought direct from step to step. Many stories and anecdotes in the newspapers and magazines provide excellent material. In the choice of books, I have found books written for children most available, as the style is apt to be simpler, more natural, more direct than those written for adults.

I advise beginning with short stories or anecdotes of about 100 to 150 words. I give a story here as an example:

A LESSON IN PHYSIOLOGY

A teacher was explaining to her class what an organ of the body is. She told them that an organ of the body is a part of the body set apart for some special use. For example, the eye is the organ of sight, the ear of hearing, etc.

After she had gone over the work pretty thoroughly, she wanted to find out how much her pupils knew of the subject. So she asked them who could tell what an organ of the body really is.

For some time there was no reply. Then

the smallest boy in the room held up his hand. "I know," he said. "I see with my eye-organ, I hear with my ear-organ, I smell with my nose-organ, I eat with my mouth-organ, and I feel with my hand-organ."

The steps for the student to follow in practising this story are as follows:

(1) Read the story over once to yourself. The help of memory is necessary to some beginners if the story be practised in the "natural" way. To follow reading is much harder than to follow conversation; some can never follow reading unless helped by memory, though they may be able to understand conversation readily. In conversation the mind more or less consciously anticipates the thought, and sometimes even the words. In the reading-practise with stories, the memory helps the mind to do this. But memory should not help any more than may be necessary; and so, if you find that memory seems to help very much, read the selected story one day and practise it the next, and after a while you may even try practising a story you have read a week before, or even without reading it at all.

(2) Have some friend or assistant read the

story to you, in a tone so low that you do not hear a sound. First your assistant should read the story to himself to gain familiarity with it, and then in reading to you should read as he would talk, that is, in the colloquial rather than the recitative style. On this first reading, you should endeavor, with the help of your memory and of the words you may see here and there, to follow the general thought of the story. Do not interrupt the reader, but let him read the story to the end, whether you understand much or little. Should you, at the end, have understood very little, read the story again to yourself and try once more in the same way, that is without interruption. If, however, you succeed in following the general thought, then

(3) Let the story be read to you again, and this time you should interrupt if you do not get the *thought* of every sentence and every clause. In which case the whole sentence or clause should be repeated for you. Do not, however, interrupt for every word, provided you have seen enough of the words to get the idea of the sentence. It is necessary to train the mind in the habit of grasping the whole

from the parts, and there is no better way for a beginner to do it than by using stories in this manner. If after two or three trials you fail to understand the thought, your assistant should let you read the printed sentence, and then you should try it again.*

(4) By this time memory will be helping you considerably, and with such help you should try for absolute verbal accuracy as the story is read to you again. Do not, however, try to understand word by word as you go along, but continue to try for the sentence or clause as a whole; if the thought, aided by your visual memory, does not suggest to you every word in the sentence, let it be repeated. But do not interrupt in the middle of a clause, for frequently the latter part of it will give you the clue to the whole. And again, do not repeat the sentences after your assistant; the habit of repetition is in itself a bad habit, but is especially bad in that it tends to effect the worse habit of demanding a literal word-by-word accuracy before anything is understood at all; that is, it places the emphasis on the words instead of upon the thought. But it is yours to be honest with yourself

*Your assistant should express the same thought in other words or give you a clue word before showing you the printed sentence.

and with your assistant and to let him know if you are not *sure* you understand, so that he can repeat until you are sure. He, in repeating, should say, not the single words you may have failed to see, but always the whole clause, the purpose being to have these words suggested to the mind by the natural thought association rather than by word formations.

(5) The next step is to have the story read very rapidly to you; the aim is to train the eye and mind to quick comprehension; for such comprehension is absolutely essential to the successful understanding of conversation. You should interrupt for the thought, though by this time you ought to be able to see almost everything, for memory will be helping greatly. But the value of this rapid practise is not lost even though you know the story by heart.

(6) Now, closing the book, your assistant should tell you the story in his own words. Let him add detail and give as much change in the wording as he can. As an example, I give herewith "A Lesson in Physiology" thus changed:

A teacher was talking to her pupils about the different organs of the body. She told

them that an organ of the body is a special
part of the body. And she told them very
carefully about the eyes, and the ears, the
nose, the mouth, and the hand. And then,
after she had told them all about it, she wanted
to find out how much they remembered. So
she asked them. But nobody replied.

"Oh!" she said, "I am sure some of you
must know what an organ of the body is.
Come now, all who know raise your hands."

The smallest boy in the room put his hand
up. "I know, teacher," he said.

"Well, tell us then," said the teacher.
"What is an organ of the body?"

And the boy replied: "I smell with my nose-
organ, I see with my eye-organ, I hear with
my ear-organ, I eat with my mouth-organ,
and I feel with my hand-organ."

As in the previous work, you should always
try to grasp the sentence, or the thought, as a
whole. Do not repeat after your assistant;
but interrupt if you fail to understand, and
let him repeat. Perhaps at first you may find
the changed wording more difficult than the
original story with which you are familiar.
But surely in time you will find your assistant's

own wording easier than the original form,
which is always a good sign. For it *is* easier,
and if you are really reading the lips and not
simply following from your memory of the
words, you ought to understand the colloquial
form better than the written.

(7) Questions are an important part of
conversation; practise in answering questions
therefore is essential. This practise is readily
given by basing the questions on the story.
The questions should be natural, and at first
rather simple. The words and the phrases
of the story may well be re-used in forming
the questions.* You should not endeavor to
repeat the question after your assistant;
to do so would require a word-for-word understanding of it. But such an understanding
is not necessary in order to answer a great
many questions; if a few words suggesting
the thought be grasped, the question can
be answered intelligently. This is so over
and over again in conversation, and therefore
it is the habit of mind, the mental attitude
toward questions, that the lip-reader should
cultivate. So always answer the question
in this practise, if only the thought be understood.

*This may be done if the words of the book make a natural question.

I give a few questions, based on the story previously quoted, as examples: What was the teacher explaining to her class? What did she tell them an organ of the body is? What examples did she give them? What did she want to find out, after she had told them all about it? How long before she had a reply? Who raised his hand at last? What did he say he saw with? What did he smell with? What did he do with his mouth-organ? How did he feel?

(Aside to your assistant: If you form your questions so that they must be answered by a statement and not by "yes" or "no," your pupil will find that he cannot "bluff" in his replies.)

(8) Still another way of practising stories is by having your assistant skip around from sentence to sentence. The chief value of this practise lies in training the mind to jump quickly from one thought to another. Therefore do not attempt to repeat the sentences after your assistant, but indicate by a nod of the head that you have understood the thought (not necessarily every word), so that he may quickly read you another sentence. If you do not understand, let him repeat.

Stories used in the ways advised are intended, not for eye-training, but to train the mind in the habits that will help you most to understand conversation. Training the mind along the right lines is even more important than training the eyes.

If you find at the first lesson that you understand the words of your assistant as well as the words of the book you should read ten stories in advance. In this case your assistant should begin the story program by telling you the story in his own words, first showing you the title and proper names. Then he should read the story with interruption for thought and follow the rest of the program as above. If you understand the words of your assistant better than the words of the book, you should not read any stories in advance.

CHAPTER VI

THE STUDY OF THE MOVEMENTS

THE labial and other formations for the different sounds appear on the face not as positions but as movements. That which is formed and gone again in 1–12 to 1–13 of a second—the average length of time for each sound formation in colloquial utterance—can hardly be called a position. And any study of the sounds as positions, that is of the sounds formed singly and held, is based on a false conception of the requirements of eye-training for purposes of lip-reading. The only true way of studying the sounds is by observing the formations as they occur in words, that is, the movements for the sounds rather than the positions. Thus, if the student wishes to study the formation of long $\overline{oo}$, he should take a word containing it, as *moon*, and concentrate his attention on the $\overline{oo}$ as he says the whole word.

There are two other reasons why the sounds should be studied in words and not singly by themselves. For not only is this the only true way of seeing the formations as movements, but also (first) it is the only true way of seeing the movements when formed naturally, without exaggeration, and (second) it is the only way to avoid for many sounds a gross mispronunciation. Almost any sound tends to be "mouthed" or exaggerated when pronounced alone, and some sounds, such as *w* and *r* cannot be correctly pronounced alone except by the expert. The tendency for the non-expert in pronouncing *w* by itself would be to say "double-yoo." But put the sound in a word, as "wet," and you do not say "double-yoo-et." The sound of *f* would tend to be "eff," but for "five" you do not say "effive." The safe, the sure way, therefore, of studying sound movements is always to study the formations as they occur in words.

A word may be said about the use of pictures * in the study of the sounds: No *movement* can be shown by a picture, hence pictures can have no value as a means of practise.

---

* It is an interesting fact that pictures of the mouth illustrating the vowel sounds were used in a book for instruction in lip-reading, by F. M. B. von Helmont, published at Sulzbach, Bavaria, 1667.

However, though all sounds are movements, vowels partake more of the nature of shapes than consonants, and these shapes can be shown by pictures. But the value of the pictures is as an aid to a clearer exposition of the vowel characteristics and not at all as a means of practise. Consonants are so purely movements, and are moreover so much more readily described than vowels, that pictures of them at the best can render no help, while on the contrary they may easily lead to false impressions.

The method of learning the movements involves, first, a clear conception of their characteristics, and, second, much practise in the observation of them. The aim of the practise is to make the recognition of the sound movements a subconscious act, that is, by much repetition to make the association of certain movements with certain sounds a habit, something which we do without the consciousness of effort or concentration. Such habits of association can be formed only by repetition in practise; when formed, the mind is left free to concentrate on the thought of the speaker, not on how he is forming his speech, but on what he is saying.

I had a letter the other day from one of my pupils, in which she said: "I certainly do very well in reading the lips, but I don't know how I do it." And there is no more necessity that she should know how than there is that the hearing should know how they hear. Those who hear know the different sounds; only in listening, they never stop to think of them. Nor should the lip-reader think of the different movements, but should concentrate on the speaker's thought.

It is analogous to the way in which we read the printed page. We do not think of each letter, nor even of each word, but rather of the thought conveyed. Should we stop and spell out each word, we should have at best only a vague idea of what we were reading. Just as we have made our knowledge and recognition of the printed letters a matter of habit, performed subconsciously, so should we endeavor to make our recognition of the sound movements.

Perfection in this ability to see the sounds is impossible, and for two reasons: First, because no two mouths are just the same, and, second, because some of the movements are so slight and quick that the eye, while it may see them sometimes, cannot be sure of always seeing them.

No two mouths are just the same; some are very easy and some are very hard, with all degrees of difficulty in between. And yet all mouths do conform to certain general laws in the formation of the movements. It is similar to the peculiarities of handwriting; while no two handwritings are the same. and while some are easily legible and some read only with great difficulty, everybody conforms, or tries to conform, to certain general laws in the formation of the letters.

The second reason why perfection in seeing the sounds is not possible is because of the great obscurity of some of the movements. The difference between vocal and non-vocal consonants is invisible in ordinary speech; "bat" and "pat," for example, look exactly the same. The obscure tongue consonants, as t, d, and n, cannot be seen with any degree of dependability. The palatal consonants, k, hard g, ng, the eye sees very rarely. Some of the vowels, as short i, short e, long a, are hard to see and the eye cannot be always certain of them.

The way to practise for these difficult

sounds is not by an exaggeration of their movements. It is a waste of time to try to make the eye see by "mouthing" what cannot be seen in ordinary conversation. The aim should be to know these difficult sounds as well as possible when pronounced naturally, but not to waste energy in striving for an impossible perfection. Also it should be to know the easier movements with an almost infallible accuracy, leaving largely to the mind the task of supplying the difficult ones from the thought of the sentence.

When studying the movements it must be remembered that this book is based on the *revelation* of the movements rather than the formation, as the lip-reader is concerned with this side of the study only. It is for this reason that the entended group of vowels (see Section III.) was chosen first and developed in the order of their simplicity. These vowels give the clearest lip movements. A vowel giving a narrow opening of the lips is readily visible, as the view is not obstructed nor the mind distracted by the tongue or teeth. The second group chosen was the relaxed, because throughout the book the principle of contrast by comparison has been followed, and only such movements as have some element in common are compared. The contrast practise is of very great value. The third group developed is the puckered. It will be noted that there are no contrast words in the lesson on long ōō, puckered-narrow. That is because the movements previously studied cannot be properly contrasted with this new movement.

CHAPTER VII

VOWELS are formed fundamentally by the tongue, but to the eye of the lip-reader they are revealed chiefly by the lips. There are three groups of vowel movements: (1) Those in which the lips at the corners tend to be drawn back or *extended;* (2) those in which the lips are neither puckered nor extended but are simply opened naturally, and are lax, or relaxed, and (3) those in which the lips tend to be rounded or drawn together, or *puckered.* Under each of these three groups are to be found in colloquial speech three widths of opening between the lips, namely, a narrow opening, a medium and a wide. The pictures of the vowels will help the student to understand the peculiarities as described.

EXTENDED VOWELS

Long ē—Extended—Narrow

For the sound of long ē, as in "keen," the lips are slightly drawn back, or *extended*, at the corners, and the opening between the upper and lower lips is *narrow*.

Short ĕ—Extended–Medium

For the sound of short *ĕ*, as in "get," the lips are slightly *extended* at the corners, and the opening between the lips is neither narrow nor wide, but is *medium*. The *a*, as in "care," also has this extended-medium movement.

Short ă—Extended–Wide

For the sound of short *ă*, as in "cat," the lips are slightly *extended* at the corners, and the opening between the lips is the *widest* of the extended vowels.

RELAXED VOWELS

Short ĭ—Relaxed–Narrow

For the sound of short *ĭ*, as in "kid," the lips have the natural or *relaxed* movement, and the opening between the lips is *narrow*.

Short ŭ—Relaxed–Medium

For the sound of short *ŭ*, as in "cut," the lips are *relaxed*, and the opening between the upper and lower lips is neither narrow nor wide, but is *medium*.

Ah—Relaxed-Wide

For the sound of *ah*, as in "cart," the lips are *relaxed*, and the opening between the lips is the widest of the relaxed vowels. Short *o*, as in "cot," usually has this relaxed wide movement.

PUCKERED VOWELS

Long ōō—Puckered-Narrow

For the sound of long ōō as in "coon," observe that the lips are drawn together or *puckered*, and that the opening between the upper and lower lips is very *narrow*.

Short ŏŏ—Puckered-Medium

For the sound of short ŏŏ, as in "good," the lips are *puckered*, but the opening between the upper and lower lips is wider than for long ōō, though still not wide; that is, the opening is *medium*.

Aw—Puckered-Wide

For the sound of *aw*, as in "cawed," the lips are slightly *puckered*, and the opening between the lips is the *widest* of the puckered vowels. Other sounds having the same movement are *o* in "orb" and usually *o* in "ore."

CHAPTER VIII

CONSONANTS

CONSONANT movements are at once easier and more difficult than the vowel movements; that is, there are seven out of eleven consonant movements that can be so well learned that the expert lip-reader sees them practically every time, and these movements are less subject than the vowels to the personal peculiarities of the speaker. But consonant movements are quicker than vowel movements, and for many of the consonant movements there are two or more sounds having the same visible characteristics. For example, *p*, *b*, and *m*, in "pie," "by," and "my," look alike, as do also *f* and *v*, in "few" and "view." This gives rise to a considerable group of so-called homophenous words, words that look very similar or alike; methods of dealing with this difficulty will be treated later.

Consonants may be divided into three groups: (1) those that are revealed by the *lip* movement, (2) those revealed by the *tongue* movement, and (3) those revealed by the context, being seen by the mind rather than by the eye.

Consonants Revealed by Lips

P, b, m—Lips-Shut

For *p*, in "pie," *b*, in "by," and *m*, in "my," the *lips* open from a *shut* position. This *shut* position is the characteristic that reveals these three sounds. It is the same for each in ordinary, rapid speech; the sounds must be told one from the other by the context.

F, v—Lip-to-Teeth

For *f*, in "few," and *v*, in "view," the center of the lower *lip* touches the upper *teeth*. Both sounds look the same and must be told apart by the context.

Wh, w—Puckered-Variable

For *wh*, in "what," and *w*, in "wet," the lips are *puckered*, very much as for long $\overline{oo}$; but the degree of puckering is more *variable*, being greater in slow and careful speech, and less in rapid colloquial utterance. (*Wh* and *w*, being consonants, are seldom confused with long $\overline{oo}$, which is a vowel, because consonants and vowels are rarely interchangeable in words; for example, though $\overline{oo}$, in "moon," looks much like w, it could not be mistaken for w, since *mwn* substituting w for *oo*, does not make a word.)

R—Puckered-Corners

For r, in "reef," before a vowel, the lips show a drawing together or *puckering* at the *corners*. The contrast of "three" and "thee" will help to show this. After a vowel, as in "arm," r tends to be slurred and will commonly show no movement whatever. If more carefully pronounced, however, it may show a slight puckering at the corners.

S, z—Tremor-at-Corners

For s, in "saw," and z, in "zone," the muscles just *outside* the *corners* of the mouth are tightened or drawn, causing a slight *tremulous* movement there. This movement is, at first, hard to see, but when once thoroughly learned it becomes comparatively easy. An additional help will be found in that the teeth are very close together, closer

than for any other sound. The movement
on the whole is very much like that for long
ē, extended-narrow; but it is very rarely
confused with the ē movement, for ē is a vowel
and *s* and *z* are consonants.

Sh, zh, ch, j—Lips-Projected

For *sh*, in "sham," *zh* (the *z*, in "azure" has
the sound of *zh*), *ch*, in "chap," and *j*, in
"jam," the *lips* are thrust forward or *projected*.

Consonants Revealed by Tongue

Th—Tongue-to-Teeth

For *th*, in "thin," and "then," the point
of the *tongue* shows either between the *teeth*
or just behind the upper teeth.

L—Pointed-Tongue-to-Gum

For *l*, in "leaf," the *point* of the *tongue*
touches the upper *gum*. Being formed within
the mouth, this sound cannot always be seen,
though the trained eye sees it frequently.

T, d, n—Flat-Tongue-to-Gum

For *t*, in "tie," *d*, in "die," and *n*, in "nigh,"
the *flat* edge of the *tongue* touches the upper

gum. This tongue movement shows even less than that for *l*; while the trained eye may see it sometimes, reliance in telling the sounds must frequently be on the context.

Consonants Revealed by Context

Y—Relaxed–Narrow

For *y*, in "yes," the lips are *relaxed* and the opening between the upper and lower lips is *narrow.* The movement, however, is so quick and so slight that in ordinary speech the eye rarely sees it. But although the sound is a hard one to see, it causes the lip-reader comparatively little trouble; this is because we do not have the sound very often. *Y*, as a consonant, occurs only before vowels, and hence never occurs at the end of a word, seldom in the middle, and usually at the beginning. But of the words that begin with *y*, there are not more than twenty-five in common use, and many of these, such as "you" and "yes," can readily be told by the association or context.

K, g (Hard), ng—Throat Movement

For *k*, in "kin," *g*, in "go," and *ng*, in "rang," a drawing up of the *throat* muscles just above the Adam's apple may sometimes be seen. But the movement is slight, and if seen at all must be seen while the eyes are on the mouth, and hence the lip-reader gets very little help from the throat. Usually these sounds must be revealed by the context.

H

For *h*, in "hat," there is no movement. *H* has the appearance of the following vowel. It must always be told by the context.

In taking up the study of the consonants the pupil, or teacher, must still keep in mind that the study is based on revelation and goes from the simple to the complex. A pure lip consonant was chosen for the first lesson, i. e., *p, b* and *m*. It is both formed and revealed by the lips and is the easiest of all the consonant movements. *Wh* and *w* might have been chosen as next in order, but as *wh* and *w* cannot be used both before and after a vowel they do not afford so large a vocabulary as *f* and *v*. The consonants formed by the tongue, being next in simplicity, were given as the second group—first those revealed by the lips, as *r* before a vowel, *s, z, sh, zh, ch* and *j*, and then those revealed by the tongue in the order of their simplicity. The last of the consonants are the "palate", which are practically invisible. Note that the three simplest diphthongs are brought in after *t, d* and *n* and before *k, g* (hard), *ng, nk* and *y*, to give a breathing spell and prevent discouragement. There are many variations and combinations of movements in the English language, but only those that are always, or predominantly, one thing or the other have been included, as *ch, j*, soft *g*, soft *c* and hard *c*, for instance, as the aim was not to confuse the mind of the pupil with too many details.

CHAPTER IX

WORD PRACTISE

To practise words simply for the sake of the words—that is, to try to memorize them as one would a vocabulary—is the least helpful form of word-study; for the analogy between the study of lip-reading and the study of a foreign language does not hold here. Certainly some good can be obtained from such practise, but it is not possible so to memorize word formations that the eye will infallibly recognize them whenever seen. Moreover, there is a better way of studying word-formations than in the study of the words by themselves, and this will be discussed in the chapter on Sentence Practise.

There are several ways of practising words, which, besides the intrinsic value they have, include any value that the endeavor to memorize the words would have too. Words may be used to train the eye in accuracy of observation of the sound formation, to train the mind in quickness of associated thought or idea perceptions, and to train both eye and mind in alertness of response. How words may be so used can best be shown by definite examples, and for that purpose I give herewith a list of words:

*sh*oot	*sh*arp	pea*ch*	pa*g*e
*sh*ould	*sh*ow	me*sh*	ocean
*sh*ort	*sh*y	ma*sh*	na*ti*on
*sh*eep	*sh*out	di*sh*	plea*s*ure
*sh*ed	*sh*ape	ru*sh*	a*z*ure
*sh*ad	dou*ch*e	har*sh*	lei*s*ure
*sh*ip	pu*sh*	poa*ch*	sei*z*ure
*sh*ut	por*ch*	pou*ch*	en*j*oy

It will be noticed that the lips-projected movement for *sh*, *zh*, *ch*, or *j*, enters into each of these words, as indicated by the italic letters, first as the initial element, then as the final element, and then as an element in the middle of the word.

The first and most obvious way of using the list given above is in the study of the lips-projected movement.* For this purpose have your assistant read the words to you, not too rapidly, while you concentrate your observation on this movement. For the present you

*For detailed directions refer to outline on page 97.

need pay no regard to the words themselves;
you should not even try for them. Simply
make sure that you see the lips-projected
movement in each word, and have any words
repeated in which you fail to see it until the
movement is clear.

Secondly, the words may be used for the
study of each movement in them. To do this,
your assistant should read a word, and when
you have shown by repetition that you have
understood it, let him read the word to you
again while you concentrate your attention on
the movement for the first sound in the word;
then again, while you concentrate on the
second movement; and again for the third
movement, and so on. For example, the first
word in the list is "shoot." First make sure
you know the word, and then as your assistant
repeats it watch for the lips-projected movement for the *sh*, then again for the puckered-
narrow movement for the long *oo*, and finally
for the flat-tongue-to-gum movement for the
t. You should not repeat the word each time;
simply watch and make sure you see each
sound. Your assistant needs to be cautioned
always to say the whole word, to say it naturally without exaggeration, and not to spell it.

So far, the work is aimed to train the eye in accuracy of observation. To train the mind in quickness of associated thought perceptions, the words may be used in sentences. Your assistant should first give you a word, and then, when you have understood it, let him compose and give you a sentence containing the word. The object is to have the sentence revolve about that word with an idea suggested by it. For example, take the first word in the list, "shoot": an idea suggested by the word would be, "Did you shoot the mad dog?" Or, "I saw a star shoot across the sky?" Or, "Did you ever shoot the chutes?" But such a sentence as, "Did you ever shoot?" would not be right, because no idea is suggested beyond the idea of shooting, and moreover, because the sentence might easily be mistaken for, "Did you ever chew?" In the work with your assistant it is advisable that several sentences be composed for each word, but for practise and example I will give one sentence each for the words in the above list:

should—Tell me what I should do.

short—My time was very short.

sheep—"Little Bo-peep lost her sheep."

shed—I wish the cat would not shed her hairs on the chairs.

shad—We had baked shad for dinner.

ship—What hour does the ship sail?

shut—Will you please shut the door?

sharp—The knife is not sharp enough.

show—Will you show me the book?

shy—She is a very shy little girl.

shout—Don't shout so loud.

shape—What is the shape of the house?

douche—I used a douche for my cold.

push—I will push you in the wheel chair.

porch—We sat out on the porch last evening.

peach—The peach is not ripe enough to eat.

mesh—The veil has a very fine mesh.

mash—Will you mash the potatoes for me?

dish—I put the dish on the table.

rush—I wish you were not always in a rush.

harsh—The man has a very harsh voice.

poach—Would you like to have me poach the egg?

pouch—The postman's mail pouch is full of letters.

page—Will you find the page for me in the book?

ocean—"My bonnie lies over the ocean."

nation—The nation celebrates its birthday on the Fourth of July.

pleasure—It will be a pleasure for me to have you call.

azure—The sky is a beautiful azure.

seizure—The custom house made a large seizure of smuggled goods.

leisure—I have very little leisure for reading.

enjoy—Don't you enjoy a good game of cards?

To use the list of words to develop quickness of response by eye and mind, it is necessary that your assistant should know the words practically by heart. He should then say the words, while you repeat them. Immediately when you have repeated a word he should give you the next word. You, too, must try to make your response as quickly as possible, the whole effort being to "hit up the speed" to the maximum. The words may be given first in order, and then skipping around, over and over, until you can maintain your quickness of response from word to word through the list.

CHAPTER X

SENTENCE PRACTISE

THE chief value of sentence practise is for mind training; but any form of practise must also have value in training the eyes. Sentences, too, can be used in such a way as chiefly to teach the eye sound and word formations. First, however, they should be used in the more obvious way of training the mind to grasp the thought. For this purpose, as soon as the student is sufficiently advanced, sentences should be used with which he is not in any way familiar either by previous practise or even reading.

As these sentences are read to you your effort should be to understand them, not analytically, but synthetically; not word by word, but the sentence as a whole. The first part of a sentence will usually be found the hardest; if, failing to understand that part, your mind stops and tries to puzzle it out, you will lose not only the first but also the last.

On the other hand, if you strive to understand the sentence as a whole, and do not let your mind stop, no matter how much may be lost, frequently the last part of the sentence may suggest the first part, and thus complete understanding is attained.

Sentences may also be used to train the mind to work along the line of natural thought-associations. As all lip-readers know, the ease of understanding is increased greatly if we have any idea of the subject of conversation. Much of conversation is a direct progression from one associated thought to another, and hence any training that helps the mind to quickness in anticipation of the idea has great value. Illustrations of the method of using sentences in this way may be drawn from the sentences used in the preceding chapter on word practise. I will give first the original sentence, and then several sentences associated with it in idea or thought.

Tell me what I should do. What shall I ever do about it? I'm sure I don't know; don't ask me.

My time was very short. How much time did you have? Only about five minutes. That wasn't long enough.

What hour does the ship sail? At 10 o'clock to-morrow morning. I'll be at the pier to say good-bye. I hope you'll have a pleasant voyage.

Will you please shut the door? I feel a draught from the hall. Is there a window open anywhere?

We sat on the porch last evening. It was rather cool, but it was a glorious night. There was no moon, but I never saw the stars shine more brightly.

I wish you were not always in a rush. I never have time to talk with you. You are always in such a hurry.

The illustrations given above are intended to be suggestive, not complete. Much further work along this line can easily be given you by a clever assistant.

The sentences should also be used to train the mind to quickness of response. The original sentences, after all the preceding practise, will be pretty well in mind. Let them be read to you now with as high a degree of speed as your ability to understand will allow. They should be read not in order, but skipping around. You should endeavor to repeat each sentence as quickly as possible.

It is permissible, in order to help create this habit of quick response, to get any help from memory that you can; that is, if you see a few of the words of the sentence and those few suggest the whole sentence, let your response be immediate, just as though you had seen everything.

Finally, sentences may be used, even better than words by themselves, to teach the eye correct word formations. Use the same sentences as before, which by now you should know almost by heart, and practise them with the mirror for each word in them. The first time you say the sentence, concentrate all your thought and attention on the first word. Try to see the word as a whole, and not the individual sounds and movements. Then say the sentence over again, and concentrate similarly on the second word; then, yet again, while you concentrate on the third word, and so on.

As an illustration, take the sentence, "My time was very short." The first time you read the sentence, you concentrate on the word "my"; then as you read it again, you concentrate on "time"; the third time on "was," etc. The *whole* sentence should always be read, and always rapidly and naturally. The word you are looking for should not be emphasized, for the value of the practise lies in learning word formations when occurring in their natural associations with other words in a sentence. For example, "was" by itself is spoken with an open or wide formation for the vowel, but in the sentence the vowel is practically eliminated, as "My time w's very short."

CHAPTER XI

MIRROR PRACTISE

THE mirror is a true aid in the study of lip-reading if it be used in the right way. It is easily possible to use the mirror in such a way as to mean a complete waste of time; or, what is worse, so to use it as to do harm. It is common to hear a student of lip-reading say, "I don't get any good from my mirror practise; I know just what I am saying." If such as these only knew it, that is exactly why mirror practise should prove helpful.

We must keep in mind the purpose of mirror practise. Lip-reading as an art comprises fundamentally two different kinds of skill: (1) the ability to recognize quickly the sound and word formations as shown by the visible organs of speech, and (2) the ability to grasp the thought of the speaker. Mirror practise is not at all intended to develop the second kind of skill; it is obviously impossible to have any practise in understanding thought by watching our own mouths in the mirror; but as a means of training the eye to know and to recognize quickly the sound and word formations, mirror practise has a peculiar value just because the student knows what he is saying, for thus he never makes a mistake; he always associates the right movement with the right sound. Really to know the movements, they must be so learned that their recognition becomes a habit; that is, something that the mind does without the consciousness of effort. In forming such a habit, it is not only essential that the desired association should be made over and over again, but also that there should be no false associations. For the student who has not a skilled teacher, mirror practise provides the best possible means of learning the movements of the visible organs of speech.

But to make mirror practise thus valuable it must be done in the right way. To say words and sentences before the mirror and watch the mouth for everything in general and nothing in particular is a waste of time. It is like the hunter who missed his shot at a deer because he "aimed for the deer" and not for some vital spot. Mirror practise must be definite if it is to have value. It is so easy to let the mind wander, to make only vague associations, that we might just as well not practise with the mirror at all unless we can find a way to fix our attention definitely and in detail upon the thing we are looking for.

A still worse evil than vagueness in connection with mirror practise arises from mouthing or exaggeration of the movements, and sometimes from mistaken pronunciation or a false formation of them. To mouth or exaggerate is to give us wrong ideas of the sound and word formations, which is not simply a waste of time, but also tends to lead us astray when reading the lips of others. And this latter evil is accentuated when we try to see the sounds by pronouncing the letters by themselves, or by spelling out the words. For example, the formation of g in "go" is nothing like the formation of the letter by itself. Spell the word, and you will see on your lips "gee-o," which certainly does not look the same as "go."

The things to avoid, then, in mirror practise are vagueness, which is a waste of time, and false associations, which are a positive harm. The things to be sought are definiteness and correct associations.

Words should be practised for each movement in them. In addition to the movements already described in Chapters VII and VIII, there are the diphthongs. See the lessons on diphthongs, pp. 207ff. We must remember also that practically every word of two syllables or more has at least one unaccented vowel. In ordinary speech these unaccented vowels are slighted or slurred, with the result sometimes of showing no movement at all, as the *o* in "prison," which appears as "pris'n"; sometimes of showing a relaxed-medium movement, as the *a* in "sofa," which appears not as "so-far," but as "so-fuh"; and sometimes of showing the relaxed-narrow movement as the first *e* in "refer," which appears not as "reefer," but as "riffur." Aways in watching, for unaccented vowels, be particularly careful not to exaggerate, but to speak naturally, and then determine for yourself what the movement is. As half at least of the vowels in ordinary speech are unaccented, it is important to get a correct idea of how these unaccented sounds appear on the lips. See also the lessons on unaccented vowels, pp. 234ff.

I give herewith a list of words in which all of the movements occur:

boom	left	save	farmer
foot	tap	above	wormy
wall	cube	dollar	moreover
rip	yoke	sofa	story
sum	coil	violin	window
sharp	pipe	fearful	fury
thief	found	wary	poorly

These words should be studied for each movement in them. To do so, proceed as follows: Say the whole word while you watch your mouth in the mirror. Do not spell the words; as, for example, "b-oo-m," but say the word, "boom." Use your voice softly; you will speak more naturally than if you use a whisper or try to form the words without sound. The first time you say the word, concentrate your attention on the first sound and its movement; then repeat the word, and concentrate on the second sound and movement; and so repeat the word for each movement. It will help you to concentrate if before you say the word each time you think definitely of what you are to look for. That is, think of the lip or tongue movements, you ought to see, and then say the word and see them. Take, for example, the word "boom." For the *b* the lips have the shut position; say "boom" and see that the lips are shut for *b*. For the *oo* the lips are puckered with the narrow opening; say the word again and see these characteristics. For the *m* the lips are shut once more; repeat the word the third time and see that. Each word should be gone over many times in this way.

The method of sentence practise with the mirror is similar to that for word practise, though not with exactly the same purpose. Words are practised for the study of the individual movements that make up the word, while sentences are to be practised for the study of the word formations that make up the sentence. And sentences are of particular value to get the effect of the unaccented vowels.

Short sentences of three to seven words provide the best material for mirror practise, though long sentences can readily be used if they are studied clause by clause. Take, for example, the opening sentence of Lincoln's Gettysburg Address. This should be divided into six clauses: "Four score and seven

years ago—our fathers brought forth on this
continent—a new nation—conceived in lib-
erty—and dedicated to the proposition—that
all men are created equal." There are from
three to seven words in each of these clauses.
Such colloquial sentences as "Where do you
live?" "The weather is very warm," "What's
the matter?" make excellent material, also,
for this practise.

Whether using short sentences or clauses
from long sentences, the method is the same.
Pronounce the whole clause or sentence as
many times as there are words in it, each time
you do so concentrating your thought on a
different word, one word at a time. The
first time you should concentrate on the first
word, the second time on the second, and
so on. But you should be particularly careful not to emphasize the word for which you
are looking. In the clause, "Four score and
seven years ago," the word "and" when
spoken, naturally is hardly more than "'nd,"
the vowel being so slurred as to be almost
lost: thus, "Four score 'nd seven years ago."
To say "Four score *and* seven years ago"
would therefore be to give a false emphasis
to the word which it would not have in ordi-

nary conversation. And the object of this practise of the words in sentences is in very important measure to accustom the eye to the natural word formations of every-day talk.

Taking this clause, then, as an example, the first time you say it you should concentrate on "four," then repeat and concentrate on "score," and so on. Try to see the word as a whole, not the individual elements. Do not speak slowly, and especially do not speak word by word. Undoubtedly it is easier for you to see the words spoken in that way, but the practise is at the same time robbed of its chief value of training the eye to see rapid word formations occurring in their natural associations with other words in a sentence.

Mirror practise as outlined above is an undoubted help in the study of lip-reading; but it is a mistake to expect skill to come from such practise alone. The full, rounded development comes from combining such mirror practise with the varied forms of practise with others. A little mirror practise every day is good, from fifteen minutes to half an hour at a time, and if it is not possible to secure an assistant, it is well to increase this time. But where practise with an assistant is possible, and the best results cannot be obtained otherwise, do not let mirror practise take so much time as to exclude you from it.

PART II

FIRST OUTLINE OF DAILY PRACTISE,
THROUGH SECTION III

WHAT may be called a full cycle of practise should consist of (1) a REVIEW of the preceding lesson, (2) the study and practise of the LESSON FOR THE DAY, and (3) the PREPARATION for the next lesson. (Of course with the first lesson there will be no review.)

As an illustration: Suppose the first story, *A Lesson in Physiology*, (Sec. I, paragraph 1), and the first movement, the *lips-shut*, for *p*, *b*, and *m* (Sec. III, paragraphs 53–56), had been studied and practised. Then that story and the words and sentences under that movement would be the REVIEW; the LESSON FOR THE DAY would be the second story, *Good Advice*, and the words and sentences under the second movement, the *extended-narrow* for long *ē* (paragraphs 57–60), as well as some conversation practise; and the PREPARATION for the next lesson would be on the third story, *The Bone of Contention*, and the words and sentences of the third movement, the *extended-medium* for short ĕ (paragraphs 61-65).

Enough time should be taken for each part of the work to do it thoroughly. The exact time cannot be prescribed, for what one person can do in one hour, another perhaps cannot do thoroughly short of two hours. The outline for practise given below, subject to changes which a teacher may make according to the needs of the pupil, should be followed step by step in the order given, except that the REVIEW and the LESSON FOR THE DAY from each section as practised with assistant may be taken consecutively if desired. It will probably take from two to three hours to complete the program; do only one hour at a time, taking up the work again later from the place left off until the whole program has been completed.

OUTLINE

A. REVIEW with assistant (all review practise should be rapid).
    I. FROM SECTION I.
        a. *The Story:*
            1. Told in different words.

2. Read very rapidly.

3. Questions based on the story.

II. From Section III.

  a. *Movement Words:*

    1. Read by assistant, and repeated by pupil, in groups of two or three as case may be, each group several times in different orders.

  b. *Contrast Words:*

    1. Read, and repeated, in groups of two.

  c. *Practise Words:*

    1. Read, and repeated, one word at a time, but skipping around and going very rapidly from word to word.

  d. *Sentences:*

    1. Read, skipping around, and rapidly from sentence to sentence.

B. Lesson for the Day

  I. From Section I.

    a. *The Story.* (For details, see Chapter V):

      1. The pupil reads story to self, preferably some time beforehand. See advice under C below.

2. Assistant reads the story to the pupil, without interruption.
3. With interruption for the thought.
4. With interruption for every word.
5. Rapidly, with interruption for thought.
6. Assistant tells the story in his own words.
7. Assistant asks questions based on the story; pupil replies.
8. Assistant reads story, skipping around, rapidly, with interruption for the thought.

(If the pupil is told to read ten stories in advance, or none at all, then the assistant should first tell the story in his own words, after showing title and proper names, and follow with steps 3, 4, 5, 7 and 8.)

9. Pupil practises the story with the mirror (see Chapter XI).

II. FROM SECTION II.
   *a. *Conversation.* Pupil and assistant have definite conversation practise (see Chap. IV). Also use occasionally the conversations in Section II.

*Conversation should be given at the end of the lesson when there is time for it, or where a pupil has special need of such practise.

III. FROM SECTION III.

  a. Assistant shows pupil, by the il-
lustrative word, the characteristics
of the new movement.

  b. *Movement Words:*

    1. Read by assistant, and repeated
by pupil, in groups of two or
three as indicated, each group
several times in different orders.

  c. *Contrast Words:*

    1. Read by assistant, and repeated
by pupil, in groups of two, each
group several times over in different orders.

  d. *Practise Words* (see Chapter IX):

    1. Assistant reads; pupil does not
repeat, but simply watches for the
special movement indicated by the
italic letters.

    2. Assistant reads and pupil repeats.
As each word is understood, the
assistant repeats it over and over
as many times as there are movements in it. The first time, the
pupil watches for the first movement, the second time for the
second, and so on.

3. Assistant reads, pupil does not repeat, but simply watches for the special movement indicated by the italic letters. If the lesson is on a consonant movement, the pupil tells whether he sees the consonant being studied at the beginning or the end of the word. If a vowel, the assistant should occasionally substitute another vowel for the one studied and the pupil should indicate when he sees the change.

4. Assistant reads and pupil repeats. As each word is understood, the assistant composes and gives a sentence containing the word. Where homophonous words are given (and such words are indicated by the small number following them, words of the same appearance being followed by the same number), the sentences alone will enable the pupil to tell which is which.

4. Assistant reads rapidly, skipping around; pupil repeats quickly.

e. *Sentences* (see Chapter X):

1. Assistant reads. As each sentence is understood, the assistant composes and gives one or two more sentences associated in thought with the original sentence.

2. Assistant reads rapidly, skipping around; pupil responds quickly.

f. Pupil practises *Movement Words*, *Contrast Words*, and *Practise Words*, with the mirror to see each movement (see Chapter XI).

g. Pupil practises *Sentences* with the mirror to see each word (see Chapter XI).

C. PREPARATION FOR THE NEXT LESSON

I. FROM SECTION I.

a. *The Story:*

1. The pupil reads the story to self, once only, and does not practise. If so read, the pupil does not re-read at time of practise with assistant. Should story practise be easy for pupil, he should read ten stories ahead. If very easy, he should not read stories to himself at all. Take one story for a lesson.

II. FROM SECTION III.

    a. Pupil studies, with the mirror, the advance movement, as shown in the word given for illustration, to see the characteristics described. Take one to two movements for a lesson.

    b. *Movement Words:*

        1. Pupil practises with mirror to see only the new movement indicated by the italic letters.

        2. Pupil practises, with mirror, the words in groups of two or three as indicated to observe the differences.

    c. *Contrast Words:*

        1. Pupil practises, with mirror, by couplets to see the differences.

    d. *Practise Words:*

        1. Pupil practises, with mirror, only to see the new movement indicated by the italic letters, not for the words themselves nor for any of the other movements.

    e. *Sentences:*

        Pupil should not practise advance sentences in any way whatever, and should endeavor if possible to get along without even first reading them to himself. If this is not possible at first, it will be later.

SECTION I

Stories are to be practised according to the directions in Chapter V. After the stories given below have all been used, material for further reading practise may readily be found in books. Those written for children, frequently afford the best material, being usually in a simple, colloquial style. The student may select books to suit his own taste, but if any of the following are on hand they will be found excellent for this kind of practise: *Æsop's Fables* (Stickney's edition preferred); Tappan's *Old Ballads in Prose;* Tappan's *European Hero Stories;* Lewis Carroll's *Alice in Wonderland;* Hawthorne's *Wonder Book* and *Tanglewood Tales;* James Baldwin's *Fifty Famous Stories;* Catherine T. Bryce's *Fables from Afar;* Josephine P. Peabody's *Old Greek Folk Stories;* Lamb's *Tales From Shakespeare.* It is not intended to limit the student to these books; they are given merely by way

of suggestion. From one to four pages should
be practised for a lesson, the number of pages
being determined by the ease with which they
are understood and by the size of the page.

A Lesson in Physiology

1. A teacher was explaining to her class
what an organ of the body is. She told them
that an organ of the body is a part of the
body set apart for some special use. For
example, the eye is the organ of sight, the
ear of hearing, etc.

After she had gone over the work pretty
thoroughly, she wanted to find out how much
her pupils knew of the subject. So she asked
them who could tell what an organ of the body
really is.

For some time there was no reply. Then
the smallest boy in the room held up his
hand. "I know," he said. "I see with my
eye organ, I hear with my ear organ, I smell
with my nose organ, I eat with my mouth
organ, and I feel with my hand organ."

—*Selected.*

Good Advice

2. There were two ladies sitting in a car. One wished to have the window shut, as she said she took cold very easily and was afraid of drafts. The other wished to have the window open, for she liked fresh air and must have it. Neither lady was willing to give in. Finally, the conductor came to them.

"Conductor," said the first lady, "if this window remains open I may get a cold. It will kill me."

"Conductor," said the second lady, "if you shut this window I may suffocate."

The conductor did not know what to do. A man who was sitting in the corner said to the conductor:

"Open the window, my dear friend. That will kill one. Then shut it. That will kill the other. Then we can have peace."

—*Selected.*

The Bone of Contention

3. "At Hale's Ford, in Virginia," said Booker T. Washington, "I used to know in my boyhood an old colored man called 'Uncle Sam.'

"During the Civil War Uncle Sam took a great interest in the conflict, but he himself did not fight. A white man took him to task about this one day.

" 'Look here, Uncle Sam,' he said, 'here are the men of the North and the men of the South killing one another off on your account. Why don't you pitch in and join them?'

" 'Mah friend,' he said, 'has you ever seen two dogs fighting over a bone?'

" 'Of course I have,' said the white man.

" 'Did you ever see the bone fight?' said Uncle Sam.

—*Selected.*

Needless Alarm

4. Anyone who has traveled on the New York subway in rush hours can easily appreciate the following:

A little man, wedged into the middle of a car, suddenly thought of pickpockets, and quite as suddenly remembered that he had some money in his overcoat. He plunged his hand into his pocket and was somewhat shocked upon encountering the fist of a fat fellow-passenger.

"Aha!" snorted the latter. "I caught you that time!"

"Leggo!" snarled the little man. "Leggo my hand!"

"Pickpocket!" hissed the fat passenger.

"Scoundrel!" retorted the little one.

Just then a tall man in their vicinity glanced up from his paper.

"I'd like to get off here," he drawled, "if you fellows don't mind taking your hands out of my pocket."

—*Selected.*

A Sword Puzzle

5. The Cross of the Legion of Honor was highly prized in the time of the first Napoleon. The Emperor one˜ day met an old one-armed soldier, and asked him where he had lost his arm. "Sire, at Austerlitz." "And were you not decorated?" "No, sire." "Then here is my cross for you; I make you chevalier." "Your Majesty names me chevalier because I have lost one arm! What would your Majesty have done if I had lost both?" "Oh, in that case, I should have made you officer of the Legion." Whereupon the soldier immediately drew his sword and cut off his other arm.

Now, there is no particular reason to doubt this story. The only question is, how did he do it?   —*Selected.*

Not Far to Go

6. A distinguished lawyer and politician was traveling on the train when an Irish woman came into the car with a big basket and bundle, and sat down near him.

When the conductor came around to collect fares, the woman paid her money, and the conductor passed by the lawyer without collecting anything. The good woman thereupon said to the lawyer:

"An' faith, an' why is it that the conductor takes the money of a poor Irish woman an' don't ask ye, who seem to be a rich man, for anything?"

"My dear madam," replied the lawyer, who had a pass, "I am traveling on my beauty."

For a moment the woman looked at him, and then quickly answered:

"An' is that so? Then ye must be very near yer journey's end."   —*Selected.*

He Told the Truth

7. The country school-teacher had been telling her pupils about the seasons and their peculiarities, and to impress their minds with the facts, she questioned them upon the points she had given.

Several questions had been put and answered, and she finally reached the stupid boy in the corner.

"Well, Johnny," she said, "have you been paying attention?"

"Yes'm," he answered promptly.

"I'm glad to hear it. Now, can you tell me what there is in the spring?"

"Yes'm, I can, but I don't want to."

"Oh, yes, you do, Don't be afraid. You have heard the other pupils. Be a good boy now, and tell us what there is in the spring."

"Wy—wy—mum, there's a frog an' a lizard an' a dead cat in it, but I didn't put 'em there. It was another boy, for I saw him do it." —*Selected.*

Franklin's Toast

8. Once in London Benjamin Franklin was dining with two friends, one of whom was an Englishman and the other a Frenchman. As three nationalities were represented, it was suggested that each of the men propose a toast to his own country. The Englishman rose first, and like a true John Bull exclaimed:

"Here's to England, the sun that gives light to all the nations of the earth."

The Frenchman responded proudly in similar vein:

"Here's to France, the moon whose magic rays move the tides of the world!"

Then Franklin rose, and with an air of quaint modesty remarked:

"Here's to George Washington, the Joshua of America who commanded the sun and the moon to stand still—and they stood still."

—*Selected.*

He Did Not Bite

9. Two English boys, who were friends of Charles Darwin, thought one day that they

would play a joke on him. They caught a butterfly, a grasshopper, a beetle and a centipede, and out of these creatures they made a strange composite insect. They took the centipede's body, the butterfly's wings, the grasshopper's legs and the beetle's head, and they glued them together carefully. Then, with their new bug in a box, they knocked at Darwin's door.

"We caught this bug in a field," they said. "Can you tell us what kind of a bug it is, sir?"

Darwin looked at the bug and then he looked at the boys. He smiled slightly.

"Did it hum when you caught it?" he asked.

"Yes," they answered, nudging each other.

"Then," said Darwin, "it is a humbug."

—Selected.

Good for Him, Anyhow!

10. "I've spanked Thomas until I can spank him no more!" exclaimed Miss Hardcastle, the geographical mistress, to Miss Manners, the mathematical mistress. "Really, my arm

quite aches from the daily chastisement of that naughty boy."

"When you want him spanked again, send him to me, then," said Miss Manners. And, sure enough, at eleven o'clock next morning Thomas appeared at the door of the mathematical mistress's class-room.

"Where have you come from?" asked Miss Manners.

"Miss Hardcastle," confessed Thomas.

"I thought so!" exclaimed the teacher; and, dropping her book, she adroitly inverted the youngster with a twist, and punished him till the room rang with shrieks and whacks.

"Now, Thomas," said Miss Manners, when she had concluded her duty, "what have you to say?"

"Please, miss," blubbered the feeling scholar, "Miss Hardcastle wants the scissors!"

—*Selected.*

UNCLE NED'S OLD AUNT

11. Down South there was an old colored man called Uncle Ned. He had worked for the same family for a great many years, ever

since the war in fact. At last one day he went
to his master and said, "Master, I'd like to
have a vacation." "What, Uncle Ned," said
his master, "you want a vacation? What do
you want a vacation for?" "Why," said
.Uncle Ned, "I want to go up to Virginia."
"Up to Virginia! What do you want to go
up to Virginia for, Uncle Ned?" "Well, I
reckon I want to see my old aunt." "Your
old aunt! I didn't know you had an old aunt
up in Virginia." "Yes, sah." "And how old
is she?" "Well, I reckon she is 110 years
old." "One hundred and ten years old!
You have an aunt up in Virginia as old as
that?" "Yes, sah." "And what is your
old aunt doing up in Virginia?" "Why, I
reckon she must be living with her grand-
mother."

—Selected.

HER VIEW OF ART

12. An old gentleman who lived not far
from the country seat of the Duke of Devon-
shire (which is open to the public when the
duke is not there) one day drove with a party

of friends to this famous residence. He took also his housekeeper, Martha, a good old soul, who had been with him a great many years.

Arriving at Chatsworth, they passed slowly through room after room of almost priceless pictures. But Martha said never a word, although it was evident that she was not missing anything. Each and every picture underwent a most rigid scrutiny, much to the amusement of the rest of the party.

At last her master turned to her and said: "Well, Martha, what do you think of it all?"

"Why," exploded Martha rapturously, "I can't see a speck o' dust anywhere!"

—*Lippincott's.*

An Absent-minded Philosopher

13. One evening in cold mid-winter, Sir Isaac Newton instinctively drew his chair very close to the grate in which a fire had just been lighted. By degrees the fire became completely kindled, and Sir Isaac felt the heat intolerable, and rang his bell with unusual violence. John was not at hand. At last he appeared, but by that time Sir Isaac was almost roasted. "Remove the grate, you lazy rascal!" exclaimed Sir Isaac, in a tone of irritation very uncommon with that amiable and placid philosopher. "Remove the grate before I'm burned to death!" "Please, your honor, might you not rather draw back your chair?" said John, a little waggishly. "Upon my word," said Sir Isaac, smiling, "I never thought of that."

—Selected.

Please Call Her

14. A dignified, middle-aged gentleman was trying to read in a crowded train. Among the passengers in the car was a lady with a very sprightly little blue-eyed girl with golden hair and an inquisitive tongue, who made friends with everyone around her. She asked the dignified gentleman numerous questions, played with his watch chain, and endeavored to determine by means of the buttons on his waistcoat whether he was rich man, poor man, beggar man, or thief.

The mother fairly beamed upon him, as she was the type of woman who cannot understand that anyone might be annoyed by *her* child. However, he was becoming nervous, and rather tired of the interruptions, and, turning to the lady, said:

"Madam, what do you call this sweet little child?"

"Ethel," replied the mother with a smile and evident pride.

"Please call her, then," said the gentleman, as he resumed his reading.

—Selected.

Guess Who Sent Them

15. George and Ethel had been married only a short time. They had had a large wedding, and had received a great many handsome presents, including the usual silverware and jewelry. Because of the prominence of the bride's family, the newspapers had commented on the number and value of the many gifts.

When they returned from their honeymoon they went to live in a pretty little cottage in

the suburbs.   A few days after they had set-
tled in their new home they received in the
mail one morning two tickets for the evening
performance at a city theatre, together with a
note which read: "Guess who sent them?"
They found it impossible to identify the
handwriting, or to guess the donor, but never-
theless they decided to use them and have a
good time.

When they reached home after a very en-
joyable evening, and switched on the lights,
they found the place stripped of jewelry and
silverware.   But on the dining room table
was another note in the same handwriting,
which read: "Now you know!"

—Selected.

PUDDIN'HEAD WILSON

16. Mutual friends of President Wilson and
Colonel George Harvey say that it is as good
as a play to watch the flashes of wit that
spring from a crossing of those two keenest
of minds.   One time when Colonel Harvey
was lunching at the White House, Mark
Twain's name came up in some connection.
The Colonel remarked casually that there

still live persons who have never heard of the great humorist. The President found this almost incredible.

"Oh, yes," the Colonel continued, "only yesterday, here in Washington, I met such a one. He was an office seeker. He declared positively he had never heard of Mark Twain. I asked him about Tom Sawyer—No, he'd never heard of him either. Nor Huck Finn? No, never. Nor Puddin'head Wilson? 'Oh, Lord, yes,' he ejaculated, 'I voted for him.'" When the President's roars of laughter had subsided Colonel Harvey continued, "'And,' added the office seeker, wistfully, 'that's all the good it done me.'"

—Selected.

WILLING TO REPEAT

17. The office boy to a large firm of publishers, when sent to one of the operative departments with a message, noticed that something was wrong with the machinery. He gave the alarm, and thus prevented much damage. The circumstance was reported to the head of the firm, before whom John was summoned.

"You have done me a great service, my boy," he said. "In future your wages will be increased $1 weekly."

"Thank you, sir," said the bright little fellow. "I'll do my best to be worth it, and to be a good servant to you."

The reply struck the chief almost as much as the lad's previous service had done.

"That's the right spirit," he said. "In all the years I have been in business no one has ever thanked me in that way. I will make the increase $2. Now, what do you say to that?"

"Well, sir," said the boy, after a moment's hesitation, "would you mind if I said it again?"

—*Philadelphia Public Ledger.*

DRESDEN GOOD NATURE

18. A stranger was one day crossing the great bridge that spans the Elbe, at Dresden, and asked a native to direct him to a certain church which he wished to find.

"Really, my dear sir," said the Dresdener,

bowing low, "I grieve greatly to say it, but I cannot tell you."

The stranger passed on, somewhat surprised at this voluble answer to his simple question. He had gone but a short distance when he heard hurried footsteps behind him, and turning round, saw the same man running to catch up with him.

In a moment his pursuer was by his side, his breath almost gone, but enough left to pant out, hurriedly: "My dear sir, you asked me how you could find the church, and it grieved me to have to say I did not know. Just now I met my brother, but I'm sorry to say that he did not know either."

—*Selected.*

The Hare and the Tortoise

19. A Hare one day made himself merry over the slow pace of the Tortoise, and vainly boasted of his own great speed in running.

The Tortoise took the laugh in good part. "Let us try a race," she said; "I will run with you five miles for five dollars, and the Fox out yonder shall be the judge."

The Hare agreed, and away they started together.

The Tortoise never for a moment stopped, but jogged along with a slow, steady pace, straight to the end of the course. But the Hare, full of sport, first outran the Tortoise, then fell behind; having come midway to the goal, he began to nibble at the young herbage, and to amuse himself in many ways. After a while, the day being warm, he lay down for a nap, saying, "If she should go by, I can easily enough catch up."

When he awoke, the Tortoise was not in sight; and, running as fast as he could, he found her comfortably dozing at their goal, after her success was gained.

—*From Stickney's edition of "Æsop's Fables," by courtesy of Messrs. Ginn and Company.*

The Fortunes of War

20. A woman of social prominence, who lived near one of the big training camps, liked to entertain the soldiers in her home. She always had one or more commissioned officers to dinner each Sunday. Among them was a young Lieutenant to whom she took an especial fancy, and he was invited to dine with her more often than the other men.

One Sunday, when she was expecting this young officer for dinner, he found at the last moment that he could not get off duty, and he sent as a substitute a private, who carried a note from the Lieutenant, explaining his inability to get away, and saying that he was sending a friend in his place.

The private presented the note to his hostess, who showed very plainly that she was not pleased with the substitute, and the atmosphere was so uncomfortable that the private had the good sense not to remain for dinner.

The next time the Lieutenant dined with this lady she took him to task for what he had done. "Why did you send a private?" she demanded. "I wanted an officer." The Lieutenant replied, much to the chagrin of his hostess: "I am sorry you did not like my friend. He is a fine fellow. Before the war I was his chauffeur." —*Selected.*

Hope Deferred

21. They sat each at an extreme end of the horse-hair sofa. They had been courting now for something like two years, but the wide gap between had always been respectfully preserved.

"A penny for your thoughts, Sandy," murmured Maggie, after a silence of an hour and a half.

"Well," replied Sandy slowly, with surprising boldness, "to tell you the truth, I was just thinking how fine it would be if you were to give me a bit of a kiss."

"I've no objection," simpered Maggie, moving over; and she kissed him plumply on the tip of his left ear.

Sandy relapsed into a brown study once more, and the clock ticked twenty-seven minutes.

"And what are you thinking about now—another, eh?"

"No, no; it's more serious now."

"Is it?" asked Maggie softly. Her heart was going pit-a-pat with expectation. "And what might it be?"

"I was just thinking," answered Sandy, "that it was about time you were paying me that penny."

—*Ladies' Home Journal.*

"FATHER WON'T LIKE IT"

22. It was noon time of a very warm day in August. A man walking home to dinner saw a small boy doing his best to pile a load of hay back on the cart from which it had fallen. The sun was beating down on the uncovered head of the poor little fellow, and his face was red from the heat and exertion.

"You can't get that hay on there alone," said the man. "Come home to dinner with me, and afterwards I will help you."

"Thank you," said the boy, "but I can't do it. My father won't like it."

"Oh come along," said the man. "You can work much better after you have had something to eat."

"No," said the boy very firmly. "My father will be angry if I do."

"I know that your father wouldn't want you to work in this heat on an empty stomach. Come along and have a good meal."

So the boy went very reluctantly, and all through the meal and after he was saying that he knew his father wouldn't like it. Finally the man said: "Well, where is your father?" And the boy replied, "He is under the load of hay." —*Selected.*

DUST ON THE ATLANTIC

23. When Mr. Knox was Secretary of State he had a colored messenger in his office who knew something of geography.

Alongside of the Secretary's desk is a great globe, standing almost six feet high. The other day Mr. Knox consulted it to see if it were really true that the sun never sets on our dominions nowadays, or to learn something else of equal importance. The Pennsylvania statesman is the pink of neatness, and was somewhat irritated to find that the big revolving ball had soiled his coat sleeve.

"William," he said sharply to the messenger, and laying his finger on the globe, "there is dust there a foot thick."

"It's thicker'n that, Mr. Secretary," replied the negro with the familiarity that comes of mingling with greatness.

"What do you mean?" demanded the premier.

"Why, you'se got your finger on the desert of Sahara."

Mr. Knox did badly at trying to suppress a smile.

"You'll find some on the Atlantic Ocean, too," he remarked as he turned to his desk.
—*Crist, in the Brooklyn Daily Eagle.*

MARK TWAIN AND WHISTLER

24. A friend of Mark Twain's tells an amusing incident in connection with the first meeting between the humorist and James McNeill Whistler, the artist.

The friend had warned Clemens that the painter was a confirmed joker, and Mark had solemnly replied that he would get the better of Whistler should the latter attempt "any funny business." Furthermore, Twain determined to anticipate Whistler if possible.

The two were introduced in Whistler's studio; and Clemens, assuming an air of hopeless stupidity, approached a just completed painting and said:

"Not at all bad, Mr. Whistler, not at all bad; only," he added, with a motion as if to rub out a cloud effect, "if I were you, I'd do away with that cloud."

"Great heavens, sir!" exclaimed Whistler, almost beside himself. "Do be careful not to touch that; the paint is not yet dry."

"Oh, I don't mind that," responded Twain with an air of perfect nonchalance; "you see I'm wearing gloves."

—*Selected.*

Mr. Choate was Obliging

25. The custom for men servants to wear evening dress has its embarrassments. When Mr. Choate was our ambassador to the Court of St. James, he was one evening attending a function at which many other diplomats were present. They of course wore full regimentals, while Mr. Choate wore the simple evening dress of the American gentleman. At a late hour he was standing by the door, when a foreign diplomat approached, and mistaking him for a servant, said to him:

"Call me a cab."

"You're a cab, sir," readily responded Mr. Choate.

The diplomat, in a high state of indignation, sought the host and complained that one of the servants had insulted him, and pointed out the offender.

"Why," said the host, "that's Ambassador Choate. Come, let me introduce you."

The diplomat was greatly chagrined, and on presentation made his apologies to the American ambassador.

"Oh, that's all right," said Mr. Choate. "But if you had only been better looking, I'd have called you a hansom cab."

—*Selected.*

A Touching Message

26. The following story is told of Mr. George Broadhurst, the playwright, who is an Englishman. After having lived a week at one of the large hotels in London, when on a visit to his native country, he was surprised on the evening of his departure, although at a very late hour, to see an endless procession of waiters, maids, porters and pages come forward with the expectant smile and empty hand. When each and all had been generously tipped, he dashed for the four-wheeler that was to carry him away.

Settling himself with a sigh of relief, he was about to be off, when a page popped his head into the window and breathlessly exclaimed:

"I beg pardon, sir, but the night-lift man

says he's waiting for a message from you, sir."

"A message from me?"

"Yes, sir; he says he cawn't go to sleep without a message from you, sir."

"Really, he can't go to sleep without a message from me?"

"No, sir."

"How touching. Then tell him, 'Pleasant dreams.'"   —*Saturday Evening Post.*

The Disciplinarian

27. There is in our navy a certain rear admiral, grave, serious-minded, conscientious, who is an excellent disciplinarian.

In his younger days he was greatly distressed by the carelessness of his charming wife. She had pinned her silk petticoat in the back until there was a great frayed place at the band. She continued to wear the petticoat, however, although her efforts to keep on pinning it at the frayed place always evoked a little storm of irritation and temper.

In vain her husband urged her to mend it. Finally he decided that the only way to reform his wife was to fill her with remorse.

So this future commander of battleships with his own hands ripped off the old frayed band and sewed on a new one. Then he took it to his wife. She was greatly moved, thanked him, kissed him, and left the room.

Presently she came back, her arms laden with garments.

"Here are a few more for you, dearest," she said. "But please don't hurry about them. Just fix them whenever you have time."

And she put seven petticoats on the chair beside him. *—Youth's Companion.*

Ready for the Summer Boarder

28. The dignified president of a well-known and flourishing New England college tells the following story at his own expense:

One summer some years ago he spent a vacation of several weeks at a farmhouse in a Maine town. The next season he received a letter from his former boarding mistress inquiring if he would like to return.

In reply he stated that he would be very glad to pass another summer vacation with her, provided some needed changes were made about the place.

"First," wrote the college president, "your maid Mary is *persona non grata,* being anything but neat and orderly in her ways, and if she is still with you I trust you will at least not allow her to wait on the table.

"Secondly, I would suggest that the sanitary conditions on your place would be greatly improved if the pigsty were moved back a few rods further from the house or done away with altogether.

"I will wait until I hear from you before deciding about coming."

The somewhat particular college president was reassured by the receipt of the following reply:

"Mary has went. We ain't had no hogs on the place since you was here last summer. Be sure and come." —*Judge.*

American Humor

29. How a piece of American humor was "managed" is told by the Rev. Dr. Hillis of Brooklyn. He, with many other American scholars, attended an educational conference at Edinburgh, and sat at dinner beside a Scotch professor.

"I have had some correspondence with Professor B., of Chicago," began the Scotchman. "Is there any possibility of your knowing him?"

"Very well," was the cordial reply, "and he happens to be sitting at the next table, the third from the end."

"Indeed!" replied the astonished Scotchman. "I have also some letters from Professor O., of the University of Michigan. Probably you know nothing of him."

"On the contrary, I know him very well. There he sits near the corner of the room; the man with whiskers and gold spectacles."

This was too much of a coincidence for the nettled metaphysician, who regarded it merely as American humor; but he went on stiffly:

"Well, sir, I have had relations with another American, a minister near New York, one Dr. Hillis——"

"Oh," laughed back the other, tapping himself on the breast, "I am he."

With a snort of indignation the Scotchman fled the room. As the New York *Tribune* explains, "American humor had been carried too far."

Division of Labor

30. "Got any work this mornin', Mistah Boyd?" asked old Billy Bulger, safe in the knowledge that no work would be entrusted to him.

"No," was the response; and then, before Billy could ask for the customary contribution: "But wait a minute. Lawyer Phillips has owed me twenty dollars for twenty years. Collect it and I'll give you half." And the merchant, knowing how bad was the debt, winked at a waiting customer.

The old man found the lawyer in the middle of a group of prospective clients and influential citizens. Thrusting through the group, he called in stentorian tones:

"Mistah Phillips, suh!"

"Well?" queried the lawyer, much annoyed.

"Mistah Boyd done tell me that you've owed him twenty dollars for about a hundred years; and he wants to know can you pay him, suh."

The lawyer hurried to Billy's side.

"You idiot," he said, "do you want to ruin my business? Here!" and he thrust a ten-dollar bill into the old man's hand.

"Well, Billy," said the merchant, "did you get it?"

The old man grinned.

"I got my half all right," he chuckled; "but you'd better look out when you go back to get your half—he's right smart hot over it, suh!"

—*Success.*

Why the Stove was Elevated

31. Two professors were one time the guests of a college chum at a hunting camp in the woods. When they entered the camp their attention was attracted to the unusual position of the stove, which was set on posts about four feet high.

One of the professors began to comment on the knowledge woodsmen gain by observation. "Now," said he, "this man discovered that the heat radiating from the stove strikes the roof, and the circulation is so quickened that the camp is warmed in much less time than would be required if the stove were in its regular place on the floor."

The other professor was of the opinion that the stove was elevated to be above the window in order that cool and pure air could be had at night.

The host, being more practical, contended that the stove was elevated in order that a good supply of green wood could be placed beneath it to dry.

After considerable argument each man placed a dollar bill upon the table, and it was agreed that the one whose opinion was nearest the guide's reason for elevating the stove should take the pool.

The guide was called and asked why the stove was placed in such an unusual position.

"Well," said he, "when I brought the stove up the river I lost most of the stove-pipe overboard, and had to set the stove up there so as to have the pipe reach the roof."

. He got the money.

—*Boston Herald.*

Miser Brown

32. I was speaking of John Wanamaker. While reproving some of his Sunday-school pupils for laughing at a deaf boy's wrong answers to misunderstood questions, he said:

"Boys, it isn't right to laugh at anyone's

affliction.   Besides, you never know when
your own words may be turned against you.
I once knew a deaf man—let us call him
Brown—who was disposed to stinginess.   He
never married; but he was very fond of society, so one day he felt compelled to give a
banquet to the many ladies and gentlemen
whose guest he had been.

"They were amazed that his purse-strings
had been unloosed so far, and they thought
he deserved encouragement, so it was arranged that he should be toasted.   One of the
most daring young men of the company was
selected; for it took a lot of nerve to frame and
propose a toast to so unpopular a man as
Miser Brown.   But the young man rose.
And this is what was heard by everyone except Brown, who never heard anything that
was not roared into his ear:

" 'Here's to you, Miser Brown.   You are
no better than a tramp, and it is suspected
that you got most of your money dishonestly.
We trust that you may get your just deserts
yet, and land in the penitentiary.'

"Visible evidences of applause made Brown
smile with gratification.   He got upon his

feet, raised his glass to his lips, and said:
'The same to you, sir.' "
—*Marshall P. Wilder, in the New York
Tribune.*

How Nye Knew North Carolina

88. The story is told of the time when Bill
Nye stood on the top of Lookout Mountain
and the guide explained that they could see
seven states from that point of view; namely,
Tennessee, Virginia, Kentucky, North Carolina, South Carolina, Georgia and Alabama.

"Where's North Carolina?" Nye inquired.

The man pointed to a place in the horizon
to which distance gave a purple hue.

"What makes you think that is North
Carolina?" Nye asked.

"Oh, we know by the direction and the
conformation of the mountains there," the
man replied.

"Well, I know that's not North Carolina,"
Nye declared, with some vehemence. "And
you know it, too, if you would stop to think.
Here is a map of the United States, and you
can see that North Carolina is pink. Besides,
I know it is pink. I live in that State con-

siderably, and I have helped to paint it red, but of course I go away sometimes, and it fades a little, leaving it pink. No, sir; you can't stuff me. The place you are pointing to a color-blind man could see is purple."

Nye said those things so seriously that the man was almost dazed. He gave Nye a puzzled look, and then went on pointing out the other States.

Prussian Atmosphere

34. It was during the most congested time of day at Columbus Circle, in New York City, and I stood watching a traffic cop there, fascinated. Was he wig-wagging to that bibulous looking individual over on the side-walk? What *did* his signals mean? The surging cars were massed together, moving somehow, honking, spitting.

A little flivver crawled into view. Its two occupants looked like the kind of people who have given up a big car and a chauffeur for the duration of the war. They, like everyone else, were puzzled by the policeman's signals. They stopped the flivver, and the woman driver caught the big cop's eye. She smiled inquiringly, nodded and pointed her arm towards Fifty-ninth Street, down which they apparently wished to go. Just then a big car of khaki clad youngsters behind them honked angrily. They were holding up the army!

But neither I, nor the occupants of the flivver, nor, indeed, the impatient soldier boys, were prepared for what followed. The policeman strode to the offending little car and in bellowing, menacing accents abused the astounded couple until he was breathless! He fairly shook the little car in his rage!

"Get off the road!" he yelled. "I don't care where yuh go or where yuh want to go! Kill yerselves and smash yer jitney! Can't yuh see there are *soldiers* behind yuh? Move along! Move along!"

The flivver crawled back into the traffic and went around the fountain, whence it had come. The cop turned to the soldier load and beamed. He expected approval.

I was so near to the car full of Americans in uniform that I heard distinctly what was said. A fresh faced young captain turned in his front seat.

"The poor fish thinks he's in Prussia!" he cried. "Give him the icy glare, boys!"

The khaki-filled car moved forward, almost upsetting the beaming officer of the law, and those impudent youngsters glared straight ahead. Approval? Not for the Prussian atmosphere!

—*The Woman Who Saw.*

CUTTING RED TAPE

35. During the early days of our control of the Philippines there was a War Department order against cabling to this country the names of privates in the army who were killed, or who died of cholera. As a result, if word came that Company B, of the Fifteenth Regiment, for instance, had been in battle, every mother who had a boy serving in that command went shivering with fear for six long weeks before the mails brought word whether her boy was among those who fell or not.

Jacob Riis was asked to put the case before the President and get him to cut the red tape, if possible. When Riis arrived at Oyster Bay he found the President at lunch with soldiers and statesmen. Fortunately, Riis was seated beside General Young, a fine old warrior

whom he had met before. Riis told him of
what was on his heart. The General knew
of no such order when he was in the Philippines, and they got into quite a little argument
about it, which Riis purposely dragged out
until there was a lull in the talk at the President's end of the table, and he saw the
President looking his way. Riis asked him
if he knew of the order.

"What order?" said he; and Riis told him—
told him of the mothers fretting for their boys
all over the land. He looked up quickly
at Adjutant-General Corbin, who sat right
opposite. It was what Riis wanted. *He*
knew.

"General," said Mr. Roosevelt, "is there
such an order?"

"Yes, Mr. President," said he, "there is."

"Why?" said Mr. Roosevelt, who is a man
of few words.

General Corbin explained that the telegraph
tolls were heavy. An officer had a code word,
just one, to pay for, whereas to send the whole
name and place of a private soldier by cable
might easily cost twenty-five dollars. The
President heard him out.

"Corbin," he said, "can you telegraph from here to the Philippines?"

The General thought he might wait until he got to Washington; he was going in an hour.

"No," said the President; "no, we will not wait. Send the order to have the names telegraphed now. Those mothers gave the best they had to their country. We will not have them breaking their hearts for twenty-five dollars or fifty. Save the money somewhere else."

—*Roosevelt the Citizen,*
By Jacob Riis.

SECTION II

36. The conversations given below are not at all intended to take the place of the conversation practise directed in Chapter IV; they are rather supplementary thereto. They give many of the commonplaces of every day conversation; and the more such commonplaces are practised and memorized the better for the lip-reader.

The conversations are arranged in double column to facilitate practise. The assistant should take the part of *A*, and the pupil the part of *B*. *A*'s column in the pupil's book should be covered with a piece of paper. When the pupil has understood *A*'s remark, as spoken by the assistant, he should read *B*'s remark from the book, and so on in turn until the conversation has been successfully completed. It may be necessary to repeat the whole several times to attain the effect of easy conversation; if necessary, do so. Then

the parts should be reversed, the pupil taking
A and the assistant *B*, the pupil now covering
B's part, but otherwise practising in the same
manner as before. Finally the assistant may
take both parts while the pupil follows.

The Weather

37. A. Is this cold enough for you?

B. Plenty. My thermometer this morning was seven below zero.

A. So? Mine was only five below.

B. My house is more exposed than yours, you know.

A. Do you have any trouble in keeping the house warm?

B. Not with a still cold, like this. But when it blows, we need the open fires as well as the furnace.

A. My house is always warm, we are so protected from the wind.

B. Yes, and you are warmer in summer too.

A. Well, I must say, I don't like to be cold.

B. Nobody does, but did you ever notice how people take a sort of pride in having extreme cold?

A. Yes. There is something exhilarating about it; it arouses our fighting blood.

B. And in keeping warm, there is the feeling of having won a victory.

A. I would rather have the weather seasonable; hot days in winter are unbearable.

A. I haven't had a cold for over a year.

A. I think it will be warmer by this afternoon.

A. Do you think it will snow?

A. We have surely been having beautiful weather.

A. We have had a good many snowstorms this winter.

A. The snow is certainly beautiful in the country, but in the city—.

A. Did you see the moonlight on the snow after the last storm?

A. It was almost as bright as day.

A. I guess with this cold spell the backbone of winter will be broken.

B. We are not dressed for them, and that's the way we take cold.

B. You had better knock on wood!

B. Not very much, I fear. The wind is northeast.

B. I shouldn't be surprised if it did before night.

B. Yes, seven days of sunshine since the last snow storm.

B. Seven so far, and five of them heavy.

B. In the city it gets carted away.

B. The moon was full that night when it cleared up.

B. I'll be rather glad when spring comes.

B. I shall not be sorry. I like each season when it comes, but am always glad to change to the next.

A. The fall is my favorite season. The best days of the year come in October.

B. I think the summer is mine. "What is so rare as a day in June?"

At the Breakfast Table

38. A. Good morning.

A. Did you sleep well last night?

A. I was rather restless. I think my room was too warm.

A. Not at all. I have not even a headache.

A. That is why you are late for breakfast.

A. Will you have some fruit?

A. Are you in a hurry to get down town?

A. That's good, for I don't like to eat breakfast in a hurry.

A. I like my coffee hot, but I drink it slowly.

A. Only one. I have a sweet tooth, but not for coffee.

B. Good morning.

B. Very well indeed. Did you sleep well?

B. That's too bad. I hope you don't feel any the worse for it.

B. I slept so well, I overslept.

B. Yes, I am usually down at half past seven, and now it is almost eight.

B. Yes, thank you.

B. No, not this morning.

B. Neither do I, especially when the coffee is so hot it burns your mouth.

B. How many lumps of sugar do you like?

B. I always take two lumps, and two cups of coffee.

A. Will you please pass me the cream and sugar?

A. Yes, I always do.

A. These rolls are very good this morning.

A. I wonder what is the matter with the butter we have been having lately?

A. Yes, forty-five cents a pound, I believe.

A. Sixty-five cents for absolutely fresh ones.

A. Yes. Aren't these eggs boiled very hard?

A. Would you like some fresh water?

A. I will ring the bell. (Mary, will you bring Mr. B. a fresh glass of water.)

A. The weather is very cold this morning. You had better wear your heavy coat and muffler.

A. Certainly.

B. You eat plenty of sugar on your cereal.

B. Will you please pass me the rolls?

B. They certainly are. And may I trouble you for some more butter?

B. It is a little strong, but not much. Butter is very high now, they say.

B. That is the high cost of living. How much are eggs, do you know?

B. That's awful. Is that what these eggs cost?

B. I like them hard. But I haven't any spoon. Will you pass me one?

B. If you please.

B. The water here is certainly good. It is so clear, and not a bit hard.

B. I shall, and I think I shall warm myself before the open fire for a minute, if you will excuse me.

B. Thank you. Good morning.

AT THE DINNER TABLE

39. A. You were late home from the office to-night.

A. Is it very cold out?

A. I have some good hot soup for you.

A. Tomato bisque.

A. Do you need more salt or pepper?

A. Will you have some crackers?

A. Yes, and I had two callers this afternoon.

A. Two ladies from the church. You don't know them.

A. I picked it out my-self.

A. A little of both, if you please.

A. Please. Will you have some string beans?

A. Well, here are French fried potatoes and rice.

B. Yes, I have been very busy.

B. Very. I'm not warm yet.

B. That's good. What kind is it?

B. I like that, and this certainly tastes good.

B. No, thank you.

B. Yes, please. Have you been busy all day too?

B. Who were they? Anyone I know?

B. This chicken is very tender; it almost falls apart when I carve.

B. What part will you have to-night? White meat or dark?

B. And some of the dressing?

B. Yes, I'm hungry to-night. I can eat the string beans and every-thing else you give me.

B. I do like rice, hot, with butter and salt on it.

A. And here is some fresh bread, baked to-day.

A. Yes, some of the crabapple jelly I put up last summer.

A. The baby has been very good to-day.

A. Yes, I put him to bed an hour ago.

A. Of course. And what do you think?

A. Try.

A. No, he has a tooth!

A. I knew that.

A. Here it is.

A. I made it myself.

A. You won't sleep well to-night.

B. Have you any jelly? Chicken is not complete without jelly.

B. I'd like the gravy too, if you please.

B. He's asleep by this time, I suppose.

B. Did you show him off to your callers?

B. I could never guess.

B. He talked for them.

B. Good for him. Ah, here comes the pie,— pumpkin, my favorite!

B. Is there any cheese?

B. This is the best pie Mary ever made.

B. You're a wonder. Pumpkin pie and good black coffee. I'm satisfied.

B. I'll sleep like a top.

In the Subway

40. A. Where are we?

A. We are making very poor time this morning.

B. We just passed 59th Street.

B. Yes, we have been blocked several times.

A. And I am in a hurry to get to the office too.

A. It is certainly provoking.

A. Twenty-third street? Is that so? We have to transfer at Grand Central.

A. Did you ever see the subway when it wasn't crowded?

A. The subway is supposed to make better time.

A. No, and not half the time, I think.

A. How far?

A. Eight minutes walk. It would do you good to walk it.

A. Usually, except when I'm in a hurry.

A. Over half a mile, but I like it.

A. "Grand Central." Here is where we change for the local.

A. And it's not jammed full. We'll have a seat.

B. It always happens that way.

B. I get off at your station this morning.

B. I hope the local won't be as jammed as this car.

B. Not very often. I think the elevated is less crowded.

B. But not this morning.

B. I live too far from the elevated up town.

B. About half a mile.

B. Do you ever take the elevated?

B. Like this morning! How far do you have to walk?

B. We don't walk enough, most of us, I think.

B. There's a local waiting for us, That's good.

B. Fine! I'm tired enough of hanging onto a strap for one morning.

A. Don't you usually have to do it?

A. The local is making good time.

A. I hope not.

A. That is one reason why I prefer to take it.

A. It's worth it, especially in the summer time.

A. Aren't we almost there?

B. Nine times out of ten.

B. Perhaps you won't be late after all.

B. You have better air in the elevated than we have in the subway.

B. Maybe I will get up early some morning and join you.

B. But in the winter the subway is always warm.

B. Twenty-eighth street was the last stop. Here we are!

THE COMMUTERS

41. A. The train was late this morning.

A. I haven't seen you on the 7:53 lately.

A. Do you get to the office in time?

A. What time do you have breakfast?

A. And I at half past six.

B. Yes, about five minutes. That is why I caught it.

B. No. I've been taking the 7:58.

B. If the train is on time.

B. Half past seven. I get up at quarter before seven.

B. I don't mind it now in the summer.

A. Nor I. It gets bright so early. But in the winter——.

A. Well, I get up now sometimes at half past five to work in the garden.

A. Have you much of a garden this summer?

A. Are you getting any fruit from them?

A. You have some peach trees, haven't you?

A. This is an apple year, so they say.

A. I like to work in my garden.

A. Pretty well. The dry weather has been hard on it.

A. My lawn is in bad shape too.

A. Yes, and on the garden too.

A. It does. But nothing can take the place of good soaking rains.

B. Then we have to get up earlier to fix the furnace.

B. It's daylight that makes the difference.

B. No, I have my ground mostly planted in fruit trees, you know.

B. The cherries and the summer apples have been fine.

B. Yes, four, but they are not going to bear well this year.

B. My apples are certainly promising well.

B. How is it getting along?

B. That's a fact. We haven't had much rain.

B. Do you use the hose on it?

B. That ought to help.

B. What vegetables are you raising this year?

A. Lettuce, string beans, squash, cucumbers and corn.

A. In these vegetables and enough of the beans left over for canning.

A. Not very much. She would like to, but she hasn't the time.

A. That is doing well.

A. The train came through fast to-day.

A. What train do you take out to-night?

A. That's the one I expect to take, too.

B. Does the garden supply all your needs?

B. Does your wife put up many things in the summer?

B. Mine put up over two hundred and fifty jars of one kind or another last year.

B. Why, here we are!

B. I guess we have almost made up the five minutes it was late.

B. I hope to catch the five-thirty.

B. I'll look for you.

MEETING A FRIEND

42. A. Why, how do you do?

A. Fine. It is good to see you again.

A. I thought you were lost.

A. Where have you been keeping yourself?

A. Did you go abroad last summer?

B. Very well, thank you; and how are you?

B. Yes, I haven't seen you for a long time.

B. I have almost thought so myself.

B. I have been traveling a good deal.

B. No, my plans fell through.

A. What was the trouble?

A. Well, it's good to be busy.

A. Business?

A. My business keeps me tied right here. I envy you your change.

A. I took a whole month last summer.

A. Yes, I was there for a week.

A. All well, but father. But he is better now.

A. Every week, and sometimes oftener.

A. I will. I expect to go home again for Thanksgiving.

A. How is your wife?

A. And the boy?

A. He must be getting to be a big boy now.

A. And the little girl?

A. You ought to be happy with your family.

B. I was too busy to get away.

B. I've been just about all over this country since I saw you.

B. Yes.

B. Well, I need it, for I haven't had a real vacation for over two years.

B. Did you go back home?

B. How were all the family?

B. Do you hear from them very often?

B. Remember me to them all when you write.

B. That's fine. There's no place like home to spend Thanksgiving.

B. Very well, better than she has been for some time.

B. Well, too.

B. He's almost five. We expect to send him to school next year.

B. She's just beginning to walk.

B. I am. . When are you going to get married?

A. Don't ask me! I don't even know who the lady is.

A. Well, remember me to your wife, and a kiss for the kiddies.

A. I'm sorry, but I have an engagement.

A. I'll be glad to.

A. I'll be there. So long.

B. I'll be the first to congratulate you when you do.

B. All right, say, can you come out to dinner with me to-night?

B. To-morrow night?

B. Good. Meet me at the office at five o'clock.

B. So long.

THE STRANGER ON THE STREET

I

43. A. I beg your pardon, but can you tell me what street I'm on?

A. Which way is Broadway from here?

A. I want to find Wanamaker's store.

A. And may I ask which way is down? I'm a stranger in the city.

A. Oh, I don't like to trouble you so much.

A. It is certainly very kind of you.

B. You're on 20th street.

B. That way. Cross Fifth Avenue and the next street is Broadway.

B. That's about twelve blocks down. You can take a car.

B. I'll walk with you to Broadway and put you on the car.

B. It's no trouble at all. I'm going that way.

B. There is a car coming now. Hurry if you want to catch it.

A. I thank you very much.

B. It's nothing at all. I'm glad to do it.

II

A. Pardon me, sir, but can you tell me how to find the address on this paper?

B. 600 West 129th Street. Take the subway to Manhattan Street.

A. Is it far up town, sir?

B. Yes, way up tcwn.

A. I hope it isn't very far.

B. Well, it is pretty far.

A. Can I walk it, sir?

B. If you can walk seven or eight miles.

A. I can never do that.

B. Take the subway, then.

A. I haven't any money, sir, not a cent in my pocket.

B. So that is your game, is it? I thought so. Good morning.

A. Just a minute, sir. I swear——.

B. Will you swear to spend it on a drink?

A. Oh, sir.

B. Will you?

A. Yes, sir.

B. Here's your nickel.

III

A. Excuse me.

B. Well?

A. I'm starving, sir.

B. You don't look it.

A. I am, sir. I haven't tasted a morsel of food for three days.

B. That's a long time, and I'll never let a hungry man starve if I can help it.

A. Thank you, sir. A quarter will give me food and a bed.

A. Oh, I couldn't do that, sir. You're very kind, but——.

A. You have a kind heart, sir. But I can't do it, sir.

A. Thank you, sir, but no, sir.

B. No, you come with me. I'm hungry myself. We'll have a good dinner together.

B. Oh, we won't go to a restaurant; just to a cheap lunch place.

B. You had better come along. I never give money on the street, but I'll give a square meal any time.

B. All right. Good day.

The Doctor's Call

44. A. Well, how's my patient to-day?

A. Let me see your tongue.

A. Now just slip this thermometer under it, while I feel your pulse. There, you can't use your tongue very much now.

A. How did you sleep last night?

A. Do you have any pain now?

B. I don't know. That's for you to find out, doctor.

B. It is still in good working order.

B. I'm always glad when that thermometer comes out. I feel like taking a bite out of it.

B. Not very well.

B. Some, but that is much better.

A. Open your mouth; I want to see your throat.

A. Very good.

B. Was that wide enough?

B. When are you going to let me get up, doctor?

A. To-day. You may sit up for half an hour this afternoon.

A. Much better. You have no temperature, and your pulse is normal.

A. Fresh air, sleep, and a tonic, and you will soon be well again.

A. Good; all you need now is building up.

A. I will give you a prescription.

A. I shall not come again for several days.

B. Am I really better?

B. But I still feel like a rag.

B. I always sleep with my window open.

B. What tonic shall I take?

B. Thank you. I will send it to the drugstore to be filled.

B. All right, doctor. Good-bye.

THE HOME

45. A. I shall be glad to see your new home.

A. Did you say you bought it or built it?

B. We like it very much.

B. We built. We bought the land a year ago, and built during the summer.

A. You know the proverb: "Fools build houses and wise men buy them."

B. Yes. I know; but fortunately it doesn't hold in our case.

A. How far are you from the station?

B. About seven minutes walk. We are almost there.

A. That is not far.

B. No. You can see the house now.

A. It looks well; it is very attractive from the outside.

B. And I think you will like the inside even better.

A. You have a good lot.

B. Seventy-five feet wide.

A. How deep?

B. One hundred and fifty.

A. You have a large porch.

B. Yes, it is made for comfort.

A. (Inside the house). I like the arrangement of the house very much.

B. That we think is the most important thing in building.

A. Your central hall is a favorite idea of mine.

B. A central hall and rooms at the four corners were what we insisted on.

A. How many rooms have you?

B. Nine and bath. And two unfinished rooms in the attic.

A. You use the unfinished rooms for storage, I suppose.

B. One of them. The other is a playroom for the children.

A. And you can have it finished off sometime if you want to.

B. Yes, we probably shall.—On the first floor, you see, we have parlor, library, dining-room and kitchen.

A. They all have good light.

B. Every room in the house has.

A. That's a handsome fireplace in the library.

B. Isn't it? And we have many a cheery fire there.

A. Nothing is more delightful on a cold winter evening.

B. Come upstairs, and let me show you the bedrooms.

A. Four bedrooms?

B. We use three for bedrooms. The other is my wife's sewing room.

A. You certainly have good light and ventilation.

B. Yes, cross-ventilation in every bedroom.

A. You ought to be fairly comfortable in summer.

B. We expect to be. We didn't get into the house until September.

A. Was it finished on schedule time?

B. It was to be done the first of October. We moved in a week ahead.

A. Well, you're the first one I ever heard of did that.

B. We had a good architect and a good contractor.

A. You have a fine house. I'll take back that proverb!

B. Thank you. I knew you'd like it.

At School (Useful Information)

46. A. What is the postal rate on letters in the United States?

B. Two cents for each ounce or fraction.

A. What is the rate to England?

B. The same, and also to Germany by direct steamer.

A. Are there any other foreign countries to which the rate is two cents?

B. Canada, Newfoundland, Mexico, Panama and Shanghai.

A. What is the rate to other countries?

B. Five cents for the first ounce, and three cents for each ounce additional.

A. What legal holidays are observed in all the states of the Union?

B. Only four, Washington's Birthday, Fourth of July, Thanksgiving Day and Christmas.

A. What states do not observe New Year's day?

B. Only Kansas and Massachusetts.

A. How many states are there in the Union?

B. Forty-eight.

A. Which was the last to be admitted?

B. Arizona.

A. What is the population of the United States?

B. Over ninety million at the last census.

A. What is the total area of the United States?

B. Over three million square miles.

A. Which state has the largest population?

B. New York, with over nine million.

A. Which state has the smallest?

B. Nevada, with about eighty-one thousand.

A. Who was the first president of the country?

B. George Washington.

A. How long did he serve?

B. Eight years.

A. How many terms?

B. Two terms of four years each.

A. How long is a senator's term of office?

B. He serves for six years.

A. And a member of the House of Representatives?

B. His term is for only two years.

A. What are the three departments of the government?

B. The executive, the legislative and the judicial.

A. How long do the members of the Supreme Court serve?

B. For life.

A. What country of the world has the largest population?

B. China, with a population of over four hundred million.

A. What is the Chinese form of government?

B. It is the Republican form of government.

A. What is the British form of government?

B. A constitutional monarchy.

A. What is the shortest day of the year?

B. Usually it is December 21st.

A. What is the longest?

B. June 21st.

Church

47. A. Did you have a good sermon to-day?

A. That's saying a good deal.

A. What was the text?

A. How was the attendance?

A. In spite of the storm!

A. You didn't stay to Sunday School?

A. You're home so early.

A. Was the Sunday School attendance up to the average too?

A. How was your class?

A. What is the Sunday School membership now?

A. Did you bring home a church calendar?

A. Why, Dr. Smith is going to speak at Wednesday night prayer meeting!

B. Very good, better than usual.

B. I wish you could have been there.

B. "Thou shalt love thy neighbor as thyself."

B. The church was full.

B. Yes, the storm hardly seemed to make any difference.

B. Yes, I did. What made you think I didn't?

B. The usual time, quarter after one.

B. Not quite, but very good for a stormy day.

B. Only one absent.

B. Over four hundred, and thirty on the cradle roll.

B. Yes, here it is. There are several interesting things this week.

B. I shall go surely and hope you will be able to by then.

A. So do I. The missionary meeting comes Thursday afternoon.

A. Will you take me to the Men's Club concert Friday evening?

A. All the others have been very good.

A. That's doing splendidly. It was only one hundred and fifty at the beginning of the year. Did you speak to Dr. Jones after service?

A. I'll have you to thank for that.

A. There's the bell now.

B. That is held at Mrs. Brown's, and she is so near you can surely go.

B. Indeed I will. It is the last one of the season, and they say it will be the best.

B. Dr. Jones announced that the young people's society had passed the two hundred mark.

B. Just for a minute. He inquired after you. I shouldn't be surprised if you received some of the church flowers to-day.

B. No more me than the doctor.

B. And the flowers too.

BUSINESS

48. A. How's business?

A. What's the matter? Orders falling off?

A. What's the cause of the trouble?

B. It hasn't been very good the past year.

B. Yes, badly. And some orders cancelled.

B. Politics. Too much uncertainty about the tariff.

A. That's hard luck. I suppose things will pick up after election.

A. I shouldn't think that would pay.

A. Does competition affect you very much?

A. Are your competitors faring any better than you?

A. How large is your force?

A. Nor reduced wages?

A. That's good. I'm something of a socialist you know, and I like that.

A. You're not troubled much with strikes?

A. Do you have any trouble with the labor unions?

A. Well, I hope things will look up with you pretty soon.

A. Fine. Never so good.

A. Yes, the tariff doesn't affect me.

B. We certainly hope so. We are now running at an actual loss.

B. It's better than shutting down.

B. Yes, it is pretty keen.

B. No, I think not. Business is poor generally in our line.

B. Two thousand. We haven't laid off any hands yet.

B. No, not yet, and hope we won't have to.

B. Well, it's our policy, and a good policy too.

B. Haven't had a strike for fifteen years.

B. No, not to amount to anything. We are always ready to talk things over.

B. Thank you. And how's business with you?

B. Your business is semi-professional.

B. What was your increase last year?

A. Gross or net?

B. Both, if you can tell me.

A. The gross was almost 33 per cent.

B. That's a big increase.

A. It's not bad. The net was about 25 per cent.

B. That is certainly a good showing in a bad year.

A. We think so.

B. What are the prospects?

A. Very good, but always uncertain.

B. Well, I wish you luck!

Shopping

49. A. Are you waited on?

B. No, I am not.

A. What is it that you want?

B. First, I would like to match this ribbon.

A. I'm afraid that we haven't any like that. Did you get it here?

B. Yes, I got it just before Christmas.

A. This piece is the same shade but is wider than yours.

B. That will not do. It must be the same width.

A. I have no more of the narrower.

B. Then I shall have to try to match it somewhere else.

A. Do you wish to buy some veiling?

B. Yes. I want some black with white dots.

A. How is this kind?

B. Those dots are too close together. They are bad for the eyes.

A. Yes they are. Here is something with large dots further apart.

A. Yes, here is one.

A. A yard and a quarter, I should say.

A. That is thirty-five cents.

A. This is an unusual sale of suits we are having. May I show you some?

A. I'm afraid we have not the mohair but I will show you the serge.

A. Here are two exceptional values. They have been reduced from $40 to $25.

A. Will you try on the gray one?

A. With very little alteration that will fit you to perfection.

A. But this only needs to be taken up on the shoulders, and to have the sleeves shortened.

B. That is better. Have you a mirror? I want to see if it is becoming.

B. That looks very well. How much will I need for this hat?

B. Very well. How much is it a yard?

B. All right. I will put the veil on now, and you may charge it.

B. I would like to see a dark blue serge. Size 38. And also a blue mohair.

B. You might show me some gray suits too if you have any.

B. That gray one is pretty but the blue is too fancy. I want a plain tailored suit.

B. Yes, I will slip the coat on.

B. I don't like to have my coats altered. It so often spoils the shape.

B. Please show me some others. I would rather find something that fits me better.

A. This black and white is pretty. Try it on.

B. Now that fits very well. Only the sleeves need shortening.

A. Yes. And that is a very fine suit.

A. Yes, reduced from $45.

B. Is this $25 too?

A. I will slip it on you.

B. I will try on the skirt and if it fits I will take it.

B. It is just a trifle too long, but it won't be much to shorten it.

A. No. It will be very easy.

B. I will take it. How much will the alterations be?

A. They will be three dollars.

A. What is the address?

B. Very well. Charge and send it.

B. Mrs. George French, 295 West 107th Street.

A. Thank you. Good morning.

B. Good morning.

At the Restaurant

50. A. Let's sit over by the window.

A. Yes, I see one directly in front of us.

B. Is there a vacant table for two?

B. This is very nice and cosy. Now what shall we have to eat. Some oysters?

A. I think I will have an oyster cocktail.

B. Very well, I'll have mine on the half shell.

A. They always have such good cream of celery soup here.

A. Yes, I love to nibble on them between courses.

A. I don't care for that. I prefer a plain beef steak. There is nothing like it.

A. I'll have some potatoes au gratin and some asparagus on toast.

A. Don't you like Welsh rabbits?

A. Of course not. I like them after the theatre.

A. I never have it.

A. Yes, I will have some fillet of sole.

A. I'm going to have some endive with French dressing.

A. I may not want any, so let's order that later.

B. All right. We will have some. And let's have some olives and radishes on the side.

B. How would you like some beef à la mode?

B. All right. Choose what you like. We must have some vegetables too.

B. The asparagus suits me, but not the potatoes. I hate anything with cheese in it.

B. No, I hate them. You don't want one now, do you?

B. Do you like the nightmare that follows?

B. You're lucky. Why, we never ordered any fish course. Don't you want some?

B. (To waiter) Bring us some sole after the soup.

B. That is very good, but I think I'll have Waldorf Salad. What shall we have for dessert?

B. That is a good plan.

A. Ah, here is my cocktail.

A. Delicious; I never tasted better.

A. How do you like the celery soup?

A. Yes, they are!

A. I can't stand a gloomy place in which to eat.

A. Have you decided to have any dessert?

A. I'm going to have a piece of strawberry shortcake, and then some camembert cheese with crackers and a demi-tasse.

A. That's true.

B. Is it a good one?

B. These blue points are very fine. (To waiter) You did not bring me any horseradish.

B. It is excellent, and aren't these radishes crisp and fresh?

B. This dining-room is very bright and cheerful.

B. No, food doesn't taste half so good in a dark, unattractive room.

B. No, I believe I will just have some roquefort cheese and crackers and a cup of coffee with my salad.

B. We must have a good cigar too, or our feast won't be perfect.

B. (To waiter) Bring us two Havana cigars.

At the Reception

51. A. How do you do, Mrs. Brown? You certainly are a stranger.

B. I have just returned from Palm Beach, where I went to escape the bitter weather.

A. You were very fortunate for we have had such a trying winter.

B. Yes, my husband was here most of the time and he said it was the worst weather he has ever experienced.

A. How is your husband?

B. Oh, he is very well, thank you. I hope that Mr. Avery is too.

A. He is quite well now, but earlier in the winter he was laid up with rheumatism.

B. He has had quite a number of attacks, has he not?

A. Yes, but not so bad as the last one. Oh, there is Mrs. Smith.

B. So it is. How thin she looks, or is it the style of gown she is wearing that makes her look so?

A. No. I think she has been taking a flesh reducing treatment.

B. I never had much faith in that, but it certainly has done wonders for her.

A. Have you had a cup of tea or an ice?

B. No, I haven't been able to get into the dining-room because of the crowd.

A. I am almost roasted. Do let's try to get an ice.

A. I will ask that waiter to bring us each one.

A. Yes, it is. I suppose that you have lived out-of-doors at Palm Beach.

A. Do you play Auction Bridge?

A. Nor I. In fact I don't care for any other card game at all.

A. Oh, nothing in particular. I have attended the opera as usual. We have had some very brilliant performances this season.

A. We have had some good plays too. Have you seen "The Return of Peter Grimm" or "The Garden of Allah"?

A. You will enjoy that, I'm sure. Everyone does.

A. I have an engage-

B. All right.

B. I hope that he won't forget. The service at large receptions is usually so poor.

B. Yes. We even played Bridge out on the porch.

B. Oh, yes, entirely. I don't care for straight Bridge now.

B. It does spoil one for other games. What have you been doing with yourself this winter?

B. I certainly missed it while I was South. So you cannot envy me entirely. You had that advantage.

B. I saw "The Garden of Allah" last night. It is a wonderful production. To-night I am going to see "Disraeli."

B. Yes, my husband has seen it twice and is going again with me.

B. Won't you come to

ment for dinner so I really must go.

A. Thank you. I shall come very soon. Good-bye for now.

see me? You know I'm always at home on Thursdays.

B. I shall expect you. Good-bye.

The Journey

52. A. Is this where I ask for information about Florida?

A. I don't know. I want to find out.

A. Is it a very rough trip?

A. Oh, I know I should be sea sick. I don't want to go that way.

A. What railroads are there?

A. Which is the best?

A. What time do the trains leave?

A. What time does it get there?

B. Yes, madam. Do you wish to go to Florida by boat or rail?

B. The trip on the water is very delightful.

B. Sometimes it is rather rough off Cape Hatteras.

B. You can go by rail, very comfortably and quickly.

B. The Seaboard Air Line, the Southern Railway, or the Atlantic Coast Line.

B. You can make your own choice. These time tables will interest you.

B. The Seaboard Florida Limited at 11:16 a. m.

B. Just where do you wish to go?

A. How stupid of me to forget to tell you. I want to go to Seabreeze.

B. Daytona is the station for Seabreeze. The Seaboard Limited arrives there at 3:51 p. m. the next day.

A. How about the Southern Railway? What are the times on that?

B. Their train leaves New York at 12:38 noon and arrives 8:14 p. m. the next day.

A. Oh, the Seaboard is quicker.

B. Yes, it's a famous train.

A. And what is the rate?

B. One way tickets are $29.60, round trip $57.35.

A. Do the tickets allow me any stop-over privileges?

B. The one way tickets do not, but the round trip tickets do, up to May 31st.

A. Is the rate by water any less than by rail?

B. Tickets via the Savannah line to Savannah and by rail to Daytona are $28.10 one way, or $49.90 round trip.

A. Does that include meals?

B. Yes, meals and berth on the steamer.

A. Why, that's much less expensive than by rail.

B. It's a very pleasant trip.

A. Can you tell me what the rates are at the hotels?

B. From $3.00 per day up, for single room without bath.

A. How much by the week?

B. From $21.00 per week up.

A. Is that American or European plan?

B. American plan.

A. Well, I am very much obliged to you. Can you make the reservations for me?

B. We shall be glad to, both on the transportation line and at the hotel.

A. Thank you. I will be in again tomorrow.

B. We shall be happy to serve you. Good day.

SECTION III

In the study of this section, follow directions in Chapters IX, X, and XI, and in the OUTLINE, pp. 93–100.

CONSONANTS REVEALED BY LIPS

P, b, m—Lips–Shut

53. For *p*, as in "pie," *b*, as in "by," and *m*, as in "my," the *lips* open from a *shut* position. This *shut* position is the characteristic that reveals these three sounds. It is the same for each in ordinary, rapid speech; the sounds must be told one from the other by the context.

54.　　　*Movement Words*

pea—heap
bee—ēēb
me—deem

174

55. *Practise Words*

*pea[1]	bit[4]	bought	hum[8]
bee[1]	bun[5]	weep	harm
me[1]	mud[5]	hem	loop
pet[2]	part[6]	tap	bird
met[2]	barn[6]	lamb	peep
bat[3]	boot[7]	lip	boom
mat[3]	moon[7]	up[8]	babe
pit[4]	book	hub[8]	pipe

56. *Sentences*

1. Would you like pea soup for lunch? 2. I never met you before. 3. Did you wipe your shoes on the mat? 4. That will not be a bit of trouble. 5. Did you have a bun for breakfast? 6. That is only a part of the story. 7. The boot is too small for me. 8. Have you read the book? 9. I bought a new hat. 10. Why do you weep? 11. Will you hem the handkerchief for me? 12. I thought I heard a tap at the window. 13. "Mary had a little lamb." 14. I have a cold-sore on my lip. 15. Will you go up stairs for me? 16. That will not do you any harm. 17. Will you loop the loop with me? 18. I saw you peep through the keyhole! 19. The mother held the babe in her arms. 20. The man had a pipe in his mouth.

*Words marked with the same numbers look alike on the lips and must be told by the context.

Extended Vowels

Long ē—Extended-Narrow

57. For the sound of long ē, as in "keen," the lips are slightly drawn back, or *extended*, at the corners, and the opening between the upper and lower lips is *narrow*.

58.   *Movement Words*
pea—heap
bee—eeb
me—deem

59.   *Practise Words*

bee	theme	eve[3]	peal[5]
fee	leaf	heave[3]	meal[5]
we	deep[2]	fear*	beet[6]
reap	team[2]	piece	meet[6]
seam	yield	peach[4]	peat[6]
sheep[1]	keep	beach[4]	beak[7]
cheap[1]	heap	teeth	meek[7]

60.   *Sentences*

1. I was stung by a bee or a wasp. 2. What fee does the doctor charge? 3. What shall we

* Before *r*, long *e* often has relaxed instead of extended lips, especially if the *r* is strong.

do?   4. Whatsoever a man sows, that shall
he also reap.   5. Will you sew this seam for
me?   6. "Little Bo-Peep lost her sheep."
7. What is the theme of the story? 8. You
must turn over a new leaf.   9. The river is very
deep.   10. I hope I shall not have to yield.
11. Can you keep a secret? 12. The children
are playing in the sand heap.   13. We will hang
up our stockings on Christmas Eve.   14. You
have nothing to fear.   15. Will you have a
piece of pie? 16. I would like some peach pie.
17. The baby has four teeth.   18. Did you hear
that peal of thunder?   19. Where shall I meet
you? 20. The bird has a very long beak.

Short ĕ—Extended–Médium

61. For the sound of short ĕ, as in "get," the
lips are slightly extended at the corners, and
the opening between the lips is neither narrow, nor wide, but is *medium*. The *a*, as in
"care," has also this extended-medium movement.

62.   *Movement Words*

peat, pet—heap, hep
beet, bet—eeb, ebb
meet, met—team, hem

63.   *Contrast Words*

Contrast the extended-*medium* (short ĕ) with the extended-*narrow* (long ē); notice that the lips are more open for short ĕ than for long ē.

dell—deal	fed—feed
bed—bead	red—reed
said—seed	well—wheel

64.   *Practise Words*

bell	them	ebb	smell⁴
fell	left	theft	spell⁴
well	tell²	there³	wet⁵
rest	dell²	their³	when⁵
sell¹	yell	yes	beg
cell¹	kept	wedge	pare ⁶
shell	help	breath	bear⁶

65.   *Sentences*

1. I rang the door bell twice. 2. I fell down the stairs. 3. Are you feeling well to-day? 4. I think I shall rest for awhile. 5. What will you sell the horse for? 6. I found the shell on the beach. 7. Do you know them very well? 8. I left my umbrella at home. 9. Don't tell anyone. 10. Do you know the college yell? 11. I kept very quiet about it. 12. Let me

know if I can help you. 13. When does the
tide begin to ebb? 14. I reported the theft
to the police. 15. There you are! 16. Did
you say yes or no? 17. Don't try to wedge
your way through the crowd. 18. I smell the
breath of the pine woods. 19. How do you
spell your name? 20. The weather has been
very wet. 21. I beg your pardon. 22. Will
you pare the apple for me?

Short ă—Extended–Wide

66. For the sound of short ă, as in "cat,"
the lips are slightly *extended* at the corners,
and the opening between the lips is the *widest*
of the extended vowels.

67.   *Movement Words*

peāt, pet, pat—heap, hep, hap
beet, bet, bat—eeb, ebb, ab
meet, met, mat—team, hem, ham

68.   *Contrast Words*

Contrast the extended-*wide* (short ă) with
the extended-*medium* (short ĕ); notice that
the lips are open more for short ă than for
short ĕ.

lad—led	shad—shed
sad—said	tan—ten
bad—bed	fan—fen

69. *Practise Words*

bad[1]	sap	yam	pal
pad[1]	sham[3]	cap[6]	hat[7]
mad[1]	jam[3]	cab[6]	hand[7]
man[1]	that	ham	back[8]
fat[2]	lap[4]	have	bag[8]
fan[2]	lamp[4]	has	bank[8]
whack	tap[5]	hash	map
rap	tab[5]	hath	stamp

70. *Sentences*

1. The weather has been very bad. 2. "A man's a man for a' that." 3. "Jack Sprat could eat no fat." 4. The wave struck the boat with a loud whack. 5. Did you rap on the door? 6. The tree is full of sap. 7. Would you like some strawberry jam? 8. That is all right. 9. Will you put the lamp in the window? 10. I heard a tap at the window. 11. Do you like corned beef hash? 12. The wind blew my cap overboard. 13. Would you like ham for dinner? 14. Have you ever heard that before? 15. The thief's pal was arrested.

16. Take off your hat and stay awhile.   17. A bird in the hand is worth two in the bush. 18. What time will you be back?   19. There is a map of the world hanging on the wall.

20. Don't forget to put a stamp on my letter.

_____

Consonants Revealed by the Lips—(continued)

F, v—Lip-to-Teeth

71. For *f*, as in "few," and *v*, as in "view," the center of the lower *lip* touches the upper *teeth*.

72.   *Movement Words*

pea, *fee*—heap, e*ve*
pen, *fen*—ebb, e*ff*
bat, *vat*—hap, ha*ve*

73.   *Practise Words*

fee	*fun*	cle*f*	roo*f*
fed	*farm*	ha*ve*	o*ff*
fat[1]	*food*	cli*ff*	cou*gh*
fan[1]	*foot*	lo*ve*[3]	ser*ve*[4]
vat[1]	*fawn*[2]	lu*ff*[3]	sur*f*[4]
van[1]	*fought*[2]	car*ve*	*five*[5]
fib	lea*ve*	hoo*f*	*fife*[5]

74.   *Sentences*

1. Have you paid the doctor's fee? 2. Have you fed the chickens this morning? 3. The fat is in the fire. 4. Did you ever tell a fib? 5. What fun we shall have! 6. Did you ever live on a farm? 7. The food on the farm was plain but well cooked. 8. She has a very small foot. 9. I saw a doe with her fawn at the Zoo. 10. I shall leave you for an hour. 11. The music was pitched in treble clef. 12. What will you have? 13. The cliff is one hundred feet high. 14. "'Tis love that makes the world go round." 15. Will you carve the roast beef? 16. The horse has a pebble in his hoof. 17. There is a leak in the roof. 18. I am off for my vacation. 19. I heard you cough last night. 20. Are you going bathing in the surf? 21. It is almost five o'clock.

Wh, w—Puckered–Variable

75. For *wh*, as in "what," and *w*, as in "wet," the lips are drawn together or *puckered*; the degree of the puckering is *variable*, being greater in slow and careful speec'', and less in rapid colloquial utterance. The consonants *wh* and *w* occur only before vowels.

76.   *Movement Words*

pea, fee, *wee*

pen, fen, *when*

pack, fag, *whack*

77.   *Practise Words*

weave	*whip*[2]	*what*	*wave*[4]
web	*whim*[2]	*woof*	*waif*[4]
whack[1]	*won*[3]	*wool*	*wipe*
wag[1]	*one*[3] (=*wun*) *wharf*		*wove*

78.   *Sentences*

1. I saw them weave the cloth in the loom.
2. I saw the spider weave his web across the door.   3. Did you ever see the tail wag the dog?   4. Don't use the whip on that horse.
5. Who won the boat race?   6. What do you want?   7. The woof of the cloth is very fine.
8. The cloth is all wool.   9. The ship is at the wharf.   10. An immense wave broke over the ship.   11. Wipe your hands on the towel by the door.   12. The spider wove a web across the window.

Relaxed Vowels

Short ĭ—Relaxed–Narrow

79. For the sound of short ĭ, as in "pit," the lips have the natural or *relaxed* movement, and the opening between the upper and lower lips is *narrow*.

80.   *Movement Words*

peat, pit—heap, hip
feet, fit—eve, if
wheat, wit

81.   *Contrast Words*

Contrast the *relaxed*-narrow (short i) with the *extended*-narrow (long $\bar{e}$); notice the difference between relaxed and extended lips:

if—eve   fill—feel
biff—beef   whip—weep

82.   *Practise Words*

pill[1]	sip	hip[6]	spill
bill[1]	ship[3]	him[6]	spin
mill[1]	chip[3]	whiff	pick[7]
fill	this	miss	pink[7]
will	live	wish[6]	pig[7]
rip[2]	tip[4]	which[6]	big[7]
rib[2]	dip[4]	witch[6]	mink[7]
rim[2]	give	with	

83.   *Sentences*

1. Did you take your pill after lunch? 2. That will fill the bill. 3. Where there's a will, there's a way. 4. How did you rip your sleeve?

5. You should sip the water and not drink it too fast. 6. Are you waiting for your ship to come in? 7. This will be perfectly satisfactory. 8. How long would you like to live? 9. Would you like a dip in the ocean this morning? 10. I will give you the best of everything. 11. Do you know him very well? 12. I smell a whiff of smoke. 13. A miss is as good as a mile. 14. What do you wish for most of all? 15. Will you take a walk with me? 16. Don't spill the water out of the pail. 17. Can you spin a top? 18. Did you ever pick blackberries?

Short ŭ—Relaxed—Medium

84. For the sound of short *ŭ*, as in "but," the lips are *relaxed*, and the opening between the upper and lower lips is neither narrow nor wide, but is *medium*.

85.   *Movement Words*

bit, but—hip, hub
fin, fun—if, huff
win, won

bet, but—ebb, hub
fen, fun—ĕff, huff
when, won

86. *Contrast Words*

Contrast the relaxed-*medium* (short ŭ) with the relaxed-*narrow* (short ĭ); notice that the lips are more open for short ŭ than for short ĭ.

rub—rib	love—live
sun—sin	tuck—tick

87. Also contrast the *relaxed*-medium (short ŭ) with the *extended*-medium (short ĕ); notice the difference between relaxed and extended lips.

dull—dell	lug—leg
rust—rest	just—jest

88. *Practise Words*

pup[1]	sum[3]	young.	much[7]
pump[1]	some[3]	cup[6]	doth
bump[1]	shun[4]	come[6]	dull
fudge	shut[4]	hull	rut[8]
won	thumb	up	run[8]
rub[2]	love	glove	luck[9]
rum[2]	tough[5]	us	lung[9]
sup[3]	dove[5]	mush[7]	lug[9]

89. *Sentences*

1. Will you bring me some water from the pump? 2. I have made some chocolate fudge

for you. 3. Do you know who won the race?
4. Rub your hands together to get them warm.
5. I will sup with you some other time.
6. Will you please shut the window for me?
7. "He put in his thumb and pulled out a
plum." 8. All is fair in love and war. 9. The
steak was very tough. 10. We are young only
once in our lives. 11. Will you have a cup of
coffee? 12. The ship's hull was covered with
barnacles. 13. Shall we walk up the hill?
14. Will you mend the hole in my glove?
15. You must tell us all about it. 16. How
much do you want? 17. "How doth the little
busy bee improve each shining hour?" 18. The
knife is very dull. 19. You will have to run
for the car. 20. What luck did you have
fishing?

_____

Ah—Relaxed—Wide

90. For the sound of *ah*, as in "cart," the
lips are *relaxed* and the opening between the
lips is the *widest* of the relaxed vowels.

91.   *Movement Words*

bid, bud, bard—hip, hub, harp
fin, fun, far—give, cuff, carve

bad, bard—ham, harm
fat, far—have, carve

92. *Practise Words*

part[1]	tar	scarf	march[4]
barn[1]	calm	far	hearth
farm	yard	parse[3]	cart[5]
psalm	harm	bars[3]	card[5]
sharp	palm[2]	Mars[3]	park[6]
lark	balm[2]	marsh[4]	bark[6]

93. *Sentences*

1. Did you put the horse in the barn?
2. How far is the farm from the railroad?
3. Do you know the twenty-third psalm?
4. The knife is not very sharp. 5. I saw a lark in the sky. 6. The house has a tar roof. 7. The children are playing in the yard. 8. The ocean is very calm this morning. 9. There will be no harm in that. 10. Where does the palm tree grow? 11. I wore the scarf around my neck. 12. How far shall I walk with you? 13. Can you parse the sentence? 14. Will you play the march on the piano for me? 15. Will you sweep the ashes from the hearth? 16. I forgot my calling card. 17. I am going for a walk in the park.

CONSONANTS REVEALED BY LIPS
(continued)

R (Before a Vowel)—Puckered–Corners

94. For *r*, as in "reef," before a vowel,
the lips show a drawing together or *puckering* at the *corners*. (After a vowel, as in "arm,"
r tends to be slurred and will commonly show
no movement whatever; though if more carefully pronounced it may show a slight puckering at the corners.)

95.   *Movement Words*

feed, weed, *r*eed
fed, wed, *r*ed
fag, wag, *r*ag
fin, win, *r*id
fun, won, *r*un
far, what, *r*ah

96.   *Contrast Words*

Contrast the puckered-corners movement
for *r* with the puckered-variable movement for
wh and *w;* notice the slightly larger mouth
opening for *r* and the greater degree of puckering for *wh* and *w*.

reap—weep   rip—whip
rest—west   run—won
rack—whack

97. *Practise Words*

reap[1]	rap[3]	ruff[5]	rope
ream[1]	wrap[3]	route	ripe
red[2]	rich[4]	room	free
wren[2]	ridge[4]	rook	brief
ram[3]	rough[5]	raw	brow

98. *Sentences*

1. I bought a ream of paper. 2. "Three cheers for the red, white and blue." 3. The wrap was not warm enough. 4. The soil on the farm is very rich. 5. The ocean is very rough this morning. 6. What route will you take when you go West? 7. There is always room for one more. 8. The rook builds his nest in the top of a tree. 9. The weather was cold and raw. 10. Give him enough rope and he will hang himself. 11. Cherries are ripe! 12. We are a free people. 13. My time is very brief. 14. "His brow is wet with honest sweat."

S, z—Tremor-at-Corners

99. For *s*, as in "saw," and *z*, as in "zone," the muscles just *outside* the corners of the mouth are drawn or tightened, causing a slight *tremulous* movement there. This movement is. at first, hard to see, but once thoroughly learned it becomes comparatively easy. An additional help will be found in that the teeth are very close together, closer than for any other sound. The movement on the whole is similar to that for long *ē*, extended-narrow; but it is rarely confused with the *ē* movement, for *ē* is a vowel and *s* and *z* are consonants. (Soft *c*, as in "peace," has the sound of *s*.)

100. *Movement Words*

weed, reed, seed,
wed, red, said
wag, rag, sag
win, rid, sin
won, run, sun
what, rah, sard

101. *Practise Words*

seam[1]	son[3]	bees[4]	puss
seem[1]	sun[3]	dress	pause[6]
said[2]	starve	as[5]	paws[6]
set[2]	soup	has[5]	pace
sent[2]	soon	this	mice
cent[2]	saw	fuss	pose
sash	peace[4]	farce	cows
sieve	piece[4]	moose	boys

102. *Sentences*

1. You seem very much better this morning.
2. I don't know what you said. 3. The girl
wore a blue sash. 4. You cannot carry water
in a sieve. 5. What time does the sun set?
6. Never let a hungry man starve. 7. What
kind of soup would you like for dinner? 8. I
saw you on the car last week. 9. "Let us have
peace!" 10. Your new dress is very becoming. 11. Handsome is as handsome does.
12. This is just what I want. 13. Don't make
so much fuss over nothing. 14. The play
was a very clever farce. 15. I saw the moose
come out of the woods. 16. Did you ever
read "Puss in Boots?" 17. There was a pause
in the conversation. 18. I can hardly keep
pace with you. 19. When the cat is away,
the mice will play. 20. Did you pose for the
picture. 21. "The sheep are in the meadow,
the cows are in the corn." 22. Boys will be boys.

Sh, zh, ch, j—Lips-Projected

103. For *sh*, as in "sham," *zh* (the *z* in
"azure" has the sound of *zh*), *ch*, as in "chap,"
and *j*, as in "jam," the *lips* are thrust forward
or *projected*. (Soft *g*, as in "ledge," has the
sound of *j*.)

104.   *Movement Words*

reed, seat, *sh*eet—ease, ea*ch*
red, said, *sh*ed—ess, e*dge*
rag, sag, *sh*ag—has, ha*sh*
rid, sin, *sh*in—is, it*ch*
run, sun, *sh*un—us, hu*sh*
rah, sard, *sh*ard—ars, ar*ch*

105.   *Contrast Words*

Contrast this lips-projected movement (*sh*, *zh*, *ch*, *j*) with the puckered-corners movement (*r*); notice that though the lips project for both movements the projection is less for *r*; and also notice that for *r* the corners of the mouth are more drawn.

sheep—reap   chip—rip
shed—red   shove—ruff
jam—ram   shy—rye

106. Contrast also the lips-projected movement (*sh*, *zh*, *ch*, *j*) with the tremor-at-corners movement (*s*, *z*); notice that the teeth are close together for both movements, but that the lips are projected for *sh*, *zh*, *ch*, and *j*, while for *s* and *z* the lips are rather flattened.

sheep—seem   peach—peace
jam—sap   dredge—dress
chin—sin   mush—muss

107. *Practise Words*

sheet[1]	shoot[3]	mash[5]	douche
cheat[1]	chute[3]	badge[5]	bush
shed	June[3]	patch[5]	porch
shaft	shook	pinch[6]	merge[8]
chill	jaw	pitch[6]	perch[8]
jump	reach	rush	birch[8]
sharp[2]	edge[4]	arch[7]	page
charm[2]	etch[4]	harsh[7]	poach

108. *Sentences*

1. The man will cheat you if he can. 2. I tied the horse in the wagon shed. 3. The horse fell and broke a shaft. 4. There is a chill in the air to-night. 5. The noise made me jump. 6. I wore the watch charm on my fob. 7. I saw a star shoot across the sky. 8. "What is so rare as a day in June!" 9. The tempest shook the house. 10. You have a very firm jaw. 11. Can you reach that book for me? 12. Don't sit on the edge of your chair. 13. The man had a patch on his trousers. 14. Who is going to pitch in the baseball game to-day? 15. I am in a rush to catch the train. 16. The rainbow made an arch in the sky. 17. Did you use a douche for your cold? 18. Don't beat about the

bush. 19. We sat out on the porch last evening. 20. Did you ever go fishing for perch?
21. Will you find the page for me in the book?
22. Would you like to have me poach the
egg?

Puckered Vowels

Long o͞o—Puckered–Narrow

109. For the sound of long o͞o, as in "coon,"
the lips are drawn together or *puckered*, and
the opening between the upper and lower lips
is very *narrow*. (Long o͞o, being a vowel, is
seldom confused with *wh* and *w*, which are
consonants. Example: though o͞o, in "moon,"
looks much like *w*, it could not be mistaken;
for *mwn*, substituting *w* for o͞o, does not make
a word.)

110. *Movement Words*

        beet, bit, boot—heap, hip, whom
        feet, fit, food—eve, if, hoof
                wheat, wit, wooed
                read, rid, rude
    seen, sin, soon—ease, is, ooze
    sheen, shin, shoe—teach, dish, douche

111. *Practise Words*

pool	shoe	you	whose
fool	loop[1]	coop	tooth
woo	loom[1]	who	spool
rule	tomb[2]	whom	spoon
soothe	doom[2]	hoof	spook

112. *Sentences*

1. I went swimming in the pool. 2. A fool and his money are soon parted. 3. The music may woo you to sleep. 4. Do you live by the golden rule? 5. Will you tell me what will soothe the pain in my tooth? 6. "For want of a nail the shoe was lost." 7. Did you weave the cloth at the loom? 8. Have you seen the tomb of Washington at Mt. Vernon? 9. The chicken "flew the coop." 10. Who are you? 11. Whom do you wish to see? 12. The donkey has a small hoof. 13. Whose house is this? 14. The baby has a tooth! 15. I bought a spool of thread. 16. "The dish ran away with the spoon." 17. Did you ever see a spook?

Short ŏŏ—Puckered–Medium

113. For the sound of short ŏŏ, as in "good," the lips are *puckered*, and the opening between the upper and lower lips is neither narrow nor wide, but is *medium*.

114.   *Movement Words*

boot, book
food, foot
wooed, wood
rude, rook
soon, sook—booze, puss
shoot, shook—push

bet, but, put
fen, fun, foot
wen, won, wood
reck, rug, rook
set, sun, sook—Bess, bus, puss
shed, shun, shook—mesh, mush, push

115.   *Contrast Words*

Contrast the puckered-*medium* (short o͝o) with the puckered-*narrow* (long o͞o); notice the greater degree of puckering for long o͞o.

foot—food   pull—pool
put—boot   full—fool
wood—wooed   good—coot

116. Also contrast the *puckered*-medium (short o͝o) with the *relaxed*-medium (short ŭ); notice the difference between the puckered and relaxed lips.

foot—fun	wood—won
put—but	good—gun

117. *Practise Words*

pull[1]	rook	cook	wool
bull[1]	soot*	hook	put
full	shook	puss	book
wood[2]	look	push[3]	wolf
would[2]	took	bush[3]	should

118. *Sentences*

1. A long pull, a strong pull, and a pull all together. 2. The barrel is full of rain water. 3. I would not if I could. 4. My hands are blackened with soot from the stove. 5. I shook the bottle before I took the medicine. 6. Look out of the window! 7. You took a great deal of trouble for me. 8. Too many cooks spoil the broth. 9. I'll do it by hook or by crook. 10. "Pussy cat, pussy cat, where have you been?" 11. Will you push the door open for me? 12. The sheep's wool is very heavy.

*The oo in "soot" is usually short, but may be long.

13. Don't put yourself to too much trouble.
14. What book are you reading? 15. The
wolf is at the door. 16. I should have known
better!

Aw, o in "Orb"—Puckered–Wide

119. For the sounds of *aw*, as in "cawed,"
and of the *o*, in "orb," the lips are slightly
puckered, and the opening between the lips
is the *widest* of the *puckered* vowels.

120.　　　*Movement Words*

　　boot, put, pawn—whom, orb
　　food, foot, fawn—hoof, cough
　　　　wooed, wood, walk
　　　　rude, rook, raw
soon, sook, sought—booze, puss, pause
shoot, shook, short—push, porch

　　pat, part, pawn—hap, arm, orb
　　fat, far, fawn—gaff, carve, cough
　　　　whack, what, walk
　　　　rack, rah, raw
sad, sard, sought—as, ars, awes
shad, shard, short—patch, parch, porch

121.   *Contrast Words*

Contrast the *puckered*-wide, for *o,* as in "orb," with the *relaxed*-wide, for *ah;* notice the difference between puckered and relaxed lips.

for—far   born—bard
form—farm   orb—arm

122.   *Practise Words*

pawn[1]	thought	hall	ball[3]
bought[1]	lawn	orb	bawl[3]
form	taught[2]	wharf	maul[3]
warm	taut[2]	gauze	ought[4]
raw	dawn[2]	torch	auk[5]
sought	yawn	wroth	hawk[5]
short	caught	pall[3]	

123.   *Sentences*

1. The thief took my watch to the pawn-broker. 2. It is not good form to eat with a knife. 3. We have had a very warm summer. 4. The weather was very cold and raw. 5. I sought you everywhere before I found you. 6. That is the long and the short of it. 7. I never thought of that before. 8. The lawn ought to be mowed. 9. I arose at dawn this morning.

10. What makes you yawn so? 11. I caught you that time. 12. The house has a large hall. 13. The moon is the orb of night. 14. The 'ship is at the wharf. 15. Have you enough gauze for the bandages? 16. Did you ever see a torch-light parade? 17. That makes me wroth! 18. Are you going to the ball game? 19. You ought not to do that. 20. Why do you watch me like a hawk?

Consonants Revealed by Tongue
Th—Tongue-to-Teeth

124. For *th*, as in "thin," and "then," the point of the *tongue* shows either between the *teeth* or just behind the upper *teeth*.

125. *Movement Words*

see, she, *thee*—tease, teach, tee*th*
said, shed, *then*—ĕss, edge, ĕ*th*
sad, shad, *that*—has, hash, ha*th*
sin, shin, *thin*—miss, midge, my*th*
suck, shuck, *thug*—us, hush, do*th*
ars, arch, hear*th*
noose, douche, too*th*
sort, short, *thought*

126. *Practise Words*

*th*ief	*th*ump[2]	ha*th*	nor*th*
*th*en	*th*umb[2]	pi*th*[3]	*th*ree
*th*an[1]	*th*aw	my*th*[3]	*th*rive
*th*at[1]	tee*th*	hear*th*	wor*th*
*th*in	brea*th*	boo*th*	fif*th*

127. *Sentences*

1. Procrastination is the thief of time.
2. Something is better than nothing. 3. The horse is as thin as a rail. 4. I hurt my thumb in the jamb of the door. 5. The rivers were swollen from the thaw. 6. How many teeth has the baby? 7. There is hardly a breath of air. 8. I am sure that the story is all a myth. 9. Have you a fire on the hearth? 10. Did you have charge of a booth at the fair? 11. "The north wind doth blow, and we shall have snow." 12. I will meet you at three o'clock. 13. How does your garden thrive this summer? 14. The house is worth seven thousand dollars. 15. This is the fifth time I've spoken to you.

L—Pointed–Tongue–to–Gum

128. For *l*, as in "leaf," the *point* of the *tongue* touches the upper *gum*. The movement is seen as the tongue leaves the gum.

129. *Movement Words*

she, thee, *lee*—teach, teeth, dea*l*
shed, then, *let*—edge, ĕth, e*ll*
shad, that, *lad*—hash, hath, Ha*l*
shin, thin, *lit*—midge, myth, mi*ll*
shuck, thug, *luck*—hush, doth, hu*ll*
shard, *lard*—harsh, hearth, ca*rl*
shoot, *loot*—douche, tooth, too*l*
shook, *look*—push, pu*ll*
short, thought, *lord*—north, ta*ll*

130. *Practise Words*

*l*eap	*l*arge	e*ll*	wa*ll*
*l*edge	*l*oose[3]	pa*l*	whi*l*e
*l*ash[1]	*l*ose[3]	shri*ll*	who*l*e[5]
*l*atch[1]	*l*ook	hu*ll*	ho*l*e[5]
*l*ift[2]	*l*aw	gnar*l*	scow*l*
*l*ived[2]	fee*l*[4]	coo*l*	boi*l*
*l*ump	vea*l*[4]	fu*ll*	lu*ll*

131. *Sentences*

1. Can you ieap across the brook? 2. I put the book on the window ledge. 3. The door is always on the latch. 4. I could hardly lift one foot after the other. 5. Will you have one lump of sugar in your coffee, or two?

6. The boys were flying a large kite. 7. The shoes are too loose for me. 8. Look before you leap. 9. I laid down the law to him. 10. How do you feel this morning? 11. The house has a large ell on one side. 12. She has a very high shrill voice. 13. The ship was hull down upon the horizon. 14. There is a big gnarl on the trunk of the tree. 15. She was as cool as a cucumber. 16. She gave a full account of her adventure. 17. There is a high stone wall around the grounds. 18. I will see you while I am at the shore this summer. 19. That is the whole thing in a nutshell. 20. Why do you scowl at me in that way? 21. Will you boil the potatoes for lunch? 22. There was a lull in the storm.

T, d, n—Flat–Tongue–to–Gum

132. For *t*, as in "tie," *d*, as in "die," and *n*, as in "nigh," the *flat* edge of the *tongue* touches the upper *gum*. The teeth are close together, which makes the tongue movement a difficult one to see; sometimes reliance must be had upon the context.

133.   *Movement Words*

thee, lee, *t*ea—teeth, deal, dee*d*
then, let, *t*en—ĕth, ell, E*d*
that, lad, *t*an—hath, Hal, ha*t*
thin, lit, *t*in—kith, kill, ki*t*
thug, luck, *t*uck—doth, hull, hu*t*
     lark, *d*ark—hearth, carl, car*t*
     loot, *t*oot—tooth, tool, too*t*
     look, *t*ook—pull, pu*t*
thought, lawn, *d*awn—north, tall, tau*t*

134.   *Contrast Words*

Contrast the *flat*-tongue-to-gum movement
(*t, d, n*) with the *pointed*-tongue-to-gum movement (*l*); notice (1) the wider lip and teeth
opening for *l*, and (2) that the tongue shows
more for *l*.

tea—lea	meet—meal
dive—life	white—while
dove—love	hut—hull
turn—learn	pert—pearl
noon—loon	food—fool

135. Also contrast the flat-tongue-to-gum
movement (*t, d, n*) with the tremor-at-corners

movement (*s*, *z*); notice (1) that though the teeth are close together for both movements, they are closer for *s* and *z*, (2) that *s* and *z* have the tremor-at-corners while *t*, *d*, and *n* do not, and (3) that the tongue is not visible for *s* and *z* while for *t*, *d*, and *n* it may be seen as it touches the upper gum.

team—seam	peat—peace
tie—sigh	mite—mice
ton—son	mud—muss
turf—surf	pert—purse
tooth—sooth	moot—moose

136. *Practise Words*

*t*each	*t*ub[3]	fee*t*[5]	done[8]
*t*en[1]	*d*ump[3]	fea*t*[5]	dar*n*[9]
*d*en[1]	*d*umb[3]	fe*d*	dar*t*[9]
*n*et[1]	*d*ark	pla*n*[6]	tar*t*[9]
*d*ash	*t*ool	pla*nt*[6]	frui*t*
*d*ish[2]	*t*ook[4]	fi*n*[7]	foo*t*
*d*itch[2]	*n*ook[4]	fi*t*[7]	war*n*[10]
*n*iche[2]	*t*alk	to*n*[8]	war*t*[10]

137. *Sentences*

1. Will you teach me to swim? 2. I caught the butterfly in the net. 3. You will have to

make a dash for your car. 4. The automobile went over into the ditch. 5. Did you have a tub bath or a shower this morning? 6. The thunder storm made it almost as dark as night. 7. Will you bring me a nail and a hammer from the tool chest? 8. I took a long walk this afternoon. 9. I shall have to talk the matter over with you. 10. I hope you will be on your feet again soon. 11. Have you fed the cats to-day? 12. Where are you going to plant the rosebush? 13. Your new suit is a perfect fit. 14. Now, what have you done? 15. "The Queen of Hearts, she made some tarts, upon a summer's day." 16. Are there many fruit trees on the farm? 17. You put your foot in it that time! 18. I warn you to look out for that man.

DIPHTHONGS

138. The diphthongs are $\bar{a}$, $\bar{i}$, *oy*, *ow*, $\bar{o}$, and $\bar{u}$.

Each diphthong has two elements, one of which is always more emphatic and hence more prominent or noticeable than the other. It is this emphatic element that gives the eye the clue, but it is the unemphatic element that distinguishes the diphthong from the fundamental sound.

There are three diphthongs of which the *final* element is a *puckered* movement, and there are three of which the *final* element is a *relaxed* and *narrow* movement.

DIPHTHONGS WITH PUCKERED FINAL MOVEMENT

ow

139. For *ow*, as in "how," the first movement is like that for *ah*, as in "art," the relaxed-wide; but for *ow* this relaxed-wide movement is followed by a very evident puckered movement.

140.   *Contrast Words*

Contrast this sound of *ow* with *ah;* notice the puckering of the lips for *ow* which *ah* does not have.

mouse—mars	doubt—dart
pout—part	cow—car
loud—lard	how—ha

141. *Practise Words*

mouth	shout	count[3]	south
found	thou	gown[3]	foul[4]
wound	loud	how	fowl[4]
round[1]	doubt[2]	hour	pound[5]
rout[1]	town[2]	house	bound[5]
sound	down[2]	couch	mound[5]

142. *Sentences*

1. "Open your mouth, and shut your eyes, and I will give you something to make you wise." 2. Have you found out what the trouble is? 3. Have you wound the clocks this week? 4. Do not put a square peg in a round hole. 5. Can you hear the sound of my voice at all? 6. You do not need to shout at me. 7. There was a loud knock at the door. 8. Are you going down town this afternoon? 9. Don't count your chickens before they are hatched. 10. How do you do? 11. At what hour shall I meet you? 12. "This is the house that Jack built." 13. I think I will lie down on the couch for a while. 14. "When the wind is from the south, it blows the bait in the fish's mouth." 15. The air in the room was very foul. 16. I bought a pound of candy.

Long ō

143. For long ō, as in "go," we have what may be described as a *contracting puckered* movement, beginning with a slight puckering and somewhat wide opening of the lips (like the puckered-wide for *aw*) and becoming more puckered.

144.   *Movement Words*

bough, bea*u*—ope
vow, *f*oe—cove
wow, woe
rout, rote
sound, zone—house, hose
shout, shoat—couch, coach
thou, though—mouth, both
loud, load—howl, hole
now, no—out, oat

145.   *Practise Words*

pole[1]	show	toe[3]	rose
bowl[1]	though	yoke[4]	poach
mole[1]	load[2]	yolk[4]	both
foam	loan[2]	cold	stroll
woe	lone[2]	hope[5]	boat[6]
roll	no[3]	home[5]	mode[6]
soap	know[3]	loaf	poke

146.   *Sentences*

1. You will have to pole the canoe up the stream. 2. The waves are capped with foam this morning. 3. You look very woe-begone this afternoon. 4. Did you have a roll for breakfast? 5. Soap and water will wash out the stain. 6. Will you show me what you want me to do? 7. That takes a load off my shoulders. 8. How much do you know about the matter? 9. Did you ever drive a yoke of oxen? 10. We have had a very cold winter. 11. While there is life, there is hope. 12. I bought a loaf of bread. 13. Every rose has its thorn. 14. We drove over the mountain in the stage coach. 15. Shall I poach the eggs for your breakfast? 16. Will you take a stroll along the beach with me? 17. I will row the boat across the river for you. 18. Poke up the fire if you want it to burn.

Long ū

147. The beginning element for long *ū*, as in "mute," is a very quick relaxed-narrow movement, which is followed by a very decided puckered movement, like that for long o͞o.

As a rule, the relaxed-narrow element of long $\bar{u}$ cannot be seen after the following consonants, t (tune), d (due), n (new), l (lieu), s (sue), th (thew); and then $\bar{u}$ must be told from long $\overline{oo}$ by the context.

148. *Movement Words*

bough, beau, p*ew*—cope, c*u*be
vow, foe, f*ew*
house, hose, *u*se
couch, coach, h*u*ge
mole, m*u*le
mount, moat, m*u*te

149. *Practise Words*

p*ew*	c*ue*	h*ue*[2]	h*u*ge
f*ew*[1]	f*u*me	h*ew*[2]	m*u*le
v*iew*[1]	c*u*be	*u*se	m*u*te

150. *Sentences*

1. How far is your pew from the front of the church? 2. We have a beautiful view from the porch. 3. I took my cue from you. 4. Do not fret or fume about that. 5. The blocks have the shape of a cube. 6. There were all the hues of the rainbow in the western

sky. 7. What is the use of crying over spilt milk? 8. Some men have been able to amass a huge fortune in their lifetime. 9. He is as stubborn as a mule. 10. I was mute with astonishment.

CONSONANTS REVEALED BY CONTEXT

Y—*Relaxed–Narrow*

151. For *y*, as in "yes," the lips are *relaxed* and the opening between the upper and lower lips is *narrow*. It is like the movement for short *ĭ*. The movement for *y*, however, is so quick that the eye seldom sees it; usually the sound must be revealed by the context.

Y occurs, as a consonant, only before vowels. It is not a common sound, and therefore, though difficult, it causes little trouble.

152.   *Movement Words*

lee, tea, *y*e
let, ten, *y*et
lad, tan, *y*ak
luck, tuck, *y*oung
lard, darn, *y*arn
loo, too, *y*ou
lawn, dawn, *y*awn

153.   *Practise Words*

yeast	yank	yard[1]	year
yes	young	youth	yelp
yet	yarn[1]	yawl	yolk

154.   *Sentences*

1. You will need more yeast for your bread.
2. Yes, I know I shall. 3. I am not yet ready to go. 4. Why do you yank the reins so hard?
5. I was watching the mother bird teach her young ones to fly. 6. Will you buy a skein of yarn for me? 7. We would all like to find the fountain of youth. 8. I went for a sail in the yawl. 9. It will be a year before I shall see you again. 10. Did you hear the yelp of that dog? 11. The pudding takes the yolk of one egg.

K, g (Hard), ng, nk—Throat Movement

155. For *k*, as in "kin," hard *g*, as in "go," *ng*, as in "rang," and *nk*, as in "rank," a drawing up of the *throat* muscles just above the Adam's apple may sometimes be seen. The movement is slight, and if seen at all must be seen while the eyes are on the mouth.

Usually these sounds must be revealed by the context. (Hard *c*, as in "cat," has the sound of *k*.)

156.   *Movement Words*

*tea, ye, key—eat, eke
ten, yet, get—Ed, egg
tack, yak, gag—had, hag
    tin, kid—it, ink
tuck, young, cut—hut, hug
darn, yarn, cart—art, ark
too, you, coo—toot, duke
    took, cook—good, cook
daw, yaw, caw—awed, auk

157.   *Practise Words*

keel	cart[2]	beg[4]	rink[6]
get	coon	rack[5]	rug
cat[1]	good	rag[5]	hook
can[1]	call[3]	rang[5]	walk
gift	gall[3]	rank[5]	quart
cuff	leak	rig[6]	cream[7]
card[2]	peck[4]	ring[6]	creep[7]

*This group is very difficult and you must not expect too much.

158.   *Sentences*

1. The boat was sailing on even keel.
2. What time do you get up in the morning?
3. Have you a cat at your house? 4. "The gift without the giver is bare." 5. I have lost one of my cuff links. 6. Are you going to the card party this afternoon? 7. Did you ever go hunting for coon? 8. "When she was good, she was very, very good." 9. I thought I heard you call to me. 10. Did you find the leak in the roof? 11. I was in a peck of trouble. 12. She took a very high rank at school. 13. Did you hear the door bell ring? 14. I'm as snug as a bug in a rug. 15. Hang your hat and coat on the hook. 16. Will you take a walk with me? 17. I bought a quart of milk and half a pint of cream. 18. The baby is just old enough to creep.

---

h

159. For *h*, as in "hat," there is no movement. *H* has the appearance of the following vowel. It must always be told by the context.

In the following *Practise Words*, where a word is given without the *h*, it will in each instance be homophenous to the word immediately preceding it.

160. *Practise Words*

heat[1]	have	whose[6]	howl
eat[1]	hill[4]	ooze[6]	home
head[2]	ill[4]	hook	hike
end[2]	hut	hall[7]	hail[8]
ham[3]	heart[5]	haul[7]	ale[8]
am[3]	art[5]	all[7]	hue

161. *Sentences*

1. Do you feel the heat very much? 2. What shall we eat for lunch? 3. Give the horse his head. 4. We shall have boiled ham for dinner. 5. Jack and Jill went up the hill. 6. It is an ill wind that profits nobody. 7. There is a little hut up on the mountain. 8. "Faint heart never won fair lady." 9. Will you go to the Museum of Art with me? 10. Whose house is that upon the hill? 11. The water oozed from my wet shoes. 12. I felt the fish nibble at my hook. 13. Wait for me in the hall down stairs. 14. We must haul the lumber from the dock. 15. All's well that ends well. 16. Did you hear the dog howl last night? 17. I shall be home at seven o'clock. 18. The boy scouts are going on a hike. 19. We had a hail storm this afternoon.

Diphthongs (continued)

Diphthongs with Relaxed and Narrow Final Movement

Long ā

162. For long ā, as in "late," the first movement is like that for ĕ, in "let," the extended-medium; but for long ā, this extended-medium movement is followed by a quick relaxed-narrow movement. The relaxed-narrow element is difficult to see in this diphthong; it has the effect of making ā slightly slower in formation than ĕ. Frequently, however, the two sounds must be told apart by the context.

163.   *Contrast Words*

Contrast long ā with short ĕ, noticing the slower formation for ā.

aid—end	shave—chef
bait—bet	lace—less
wail—well	bathe—Beth

164.   *Practise Words*

pail[1]	save	gave	faith
mail[1]	shame[4]	haste	ail[7]
fail[2]	shape[4]	aim	ale[7]
veil[2]	they	wave[6]	shade[8]
way[3]	lame	waif[6]	chain[8]
weigh[3]	name[5]	race	bake[9]
ray	tame[5]	page	make[9]

165.   *Sentences*

1. Will you mail my letter for me? 2. "There is no such word as fail." 3. Where there's a will, there's a way. 4. The baby was like a ray of sunlight in the house. 5. Save the pence, and the pounds will take care of themselves. 6. What is the shape of the room? 7. Have they told you all about it? 8. The horse seems to be lame in his left forefoot. 9. What is your name? 10. She gave me her name, but I have forgotten it. 11. More haste, less speed. 12. I cannot see what you aim to accomplish. 13. The wave swept me off my feet. 14. Have you ever heard of the race between the hare and the tortoise? 15. There is a page torn out of the book. 16. I have unbounded faith in you. 17. What ails

you? 18. Will you pull down the shade for me? 19. You will make the mistake of your life if you do that.

Long ī

166. For long ī, as in "pipe," the first movement is like that for *ah*, in "palm," the relaxed-wide; but for long ī, this relaxed-wide movement is followed by a quick relaxed-narrow movement.

167. *Movement Words*

pay, p*ie*—ape, *I*'m
fay, f*ie*—knave, kn*i*fe
way, wh*y*
ray, r*ye*—*i*re
say, s*i*gh—ace, *i*ce
shay, sh*y*
they, th*y*—lathe, t*i*the
lay, l*ie*—ale, *i*sle
nay, n*i*gh—aid, *I*'d
gay, g*uy*—lake, l*i*ke
hay, h*i*gh

168. *Contrast Words*

Contrast the sounds of long *ī*, and of *ah;*
notice that both begin with the relaxed-wide
movement, but that *ī* is followed by the
relaxed-narrow, while *ah* is not.

pipe—palm	light—lard
mice—mars	dine—darn
pike—park	I'm—arm

169. *Practise Words*

pie[1]	sight	kite[6]	tithe
buy[1]	shy	kind[6]	pile[7]
fight[2]	thy	high	mile[7]
fine[2]	light[4]	wipe	bite[8]
why	line[4]	hive	might[8]
ripe[3]	time[5]	wire	pine[8]
rhyme[3]	type[5]	wise	like

170. *Sentences*

1. Will you have another piece of pie?
2. "We do not want to fight, but——." 3. Why
did you not tell me before? 4. There is neither
rhyme nor reason in the matter. 5. My eye-
sight is very keen. 6. The little girl seems to
be somewhat shy. 7. Put out the light.

8. What time is it? 9. It is very kind of you to do that for me. 10. There was a high wind during the storm. 11. Wipe the slate clean and begin again. 12. The bees are buzzing around the hive. 13. I will wire you as soon as I arrive. 14. I think that would be a very wise thing for you to do. 15. She gives a tithe of her income every year. 16. The aëroplane was flying faster than a mile a minute. 17. "Good night, sleep tight, and do not let the mosquitoes bite." 18. How do you like that?

———————

oy

171. For *oy*, as in "boy," the first movement is like that for *aw*, in "paw," the puckered-wide; but for *oy*, this puckered-wide movement is followed by a quick relaxed-narrow movement.

172.   *Movement Words*

bay   buy,   b*oy*

fail, file, f*oi*l—knave, knife, c*oi*f

ray,   rye,   R*oy*

sail, side, s*oi*l—days, dice, t*oy*s

lain, line, l*oi*n—ale, isle, *oi*l

day, tie, t*oy*—cane, kine, c*oi*n

gay,   guy,   c*oy*

173. *Contrast Words*

Contrast the sounds of *oy* and of *aw;* notice that both begin with the puckered-wide movement, but that *oy* is followed by the relaxed-narrow, while *aw* is not.

boy—paw   oil—all
point—pawn   troy—draw
foil—fall   coif—cough

174. *Practise Words*

boy	soil	coil	noise
foil	loin	oil	broil
roil	toil	coif	voice

175. *Sentences*

1. The boy carried the message for me. 2. The candy was wrapped in tin foil. 3. Why do you try to roil me? 4. You will soil your clothes unless you put an apron on. 5. I bought a sirloin steak for dinner. 6. "Double, double toil and trouble." 7. She wore her hair in a coil. 8. Pour oil on the troubled waters. 9. She wore a coif on her head. 10. What was that noise I heard? 11. Will you broil the steak? 12. You have a very pleasant voice.

R after Vowel

176. As a rule, *r* after a vowel is slighted or slurred. It only rarely shows the strong puckered-corners movement that it does before a vowel. Depending upon the care with which it is pronounced, it may show (1) no movement at all, or (2) the relaxed-medium movement, "our," for example, like "ow-uh," or (3) a slight puckered-corners movement.

R, After Vowel, Showing No Movement

177. An *r*, after a vowel and before a consonant, as in "farm," usually shows no movement.

Practise Words

arm[1]	barb	orb	warm[3]
harm[1]	sharp[2]	form	warp[3]
harp[1]	charm[2]	fort	short
farm	shark	born	thorn

178.   *Sentences*

1. Were you vaccinated on the arm? 2. The farm was abandoned and overgrown with thorns. 3. Did you ever climb through

a barbed wire fence? 4. There was a sharp wind from the north east. 5. A shark swam along in the wake of the ship. 6. The moon is the orb of night. 7. Your lips form the words very well. 8. The fort was captured by the enemy. 9. "Full many a flower is born to blush unseen." 10. The wood was badly warped from the dampness. 11. "The longest way round is the shortest way home." 12. Every rose has its thorn.

R, After Vowel, Relaxed–Medium

179. A final *r* in an accented syllable, occurring after a long vowel, tends to become like short *ŭ* and to show the relaxed-medium movement; though it may show a slight puckered-corners, in which case the preceding long vowel will probably be somewhat shortened.

180. *Practise Words*

fear	rear	deer[3]	sure
peer[1]	shear[2]	dear[3]	tour
beer[1]	cheer[2]	poor[4]	pure
we're	spear	moor[4]	cure

181.   *Sentences*

1. We will show neither fear nor favor. 2. I thought I saw you peer into the window. 3. We're going away for a long time. 4. You will find a seat in the rear of the car. 5. Cheer up! The best is yet to come. 6. Did you ever try to spear eels? 7. Fresh eggs are always very dear in the winter time. 8. He was as poor as a church mouse. 9. You must be sure to tell me about everything. 10. Would you like to take a tour around the world? 11. The water from the spring is as pure and clear as crystal. 12. Do you know anything that will cure a cold?

R, *After Diphthong, Relaxed–Medium*

182. A final *r* in an accented syllable, occurring after a diphthong, tends to become like short *ŭ* and to show the relaxed-medium movement; though it may show a slight puckered-corners, in which case the preceding diphthong will tend to lose its diphthongal quality and to show only its emphatic element.

183.　　　　*Practise Words*

air	chair[3]	tire	shore
fair[1]	their	ore	lore
fare[1]	lair	four	door[6]
pare[2]	dare	pore[5]	tore[6]
pair[2]	care	bore[5]	core[7]
bear[2]	fire	more[5]	gore[7]
wear	mire	wore	our[8]
rare	wire	roar	hour[8]
share[3]	lyre	sore	sour

184.　　　　*Sentences*

1. Do you feel the air from the window?
2. Faint heart never won fair lady. 3. I cannot bear a strong light in my eyes. 4. You must wear your new dress to the reception.
5. I prefer my roast beef rare, if you please.
6. If it rains, you may share my umbrella.
7. I will take their word for it. 8. Don't you dare to do that. 9. I don't believe I care to go to the meeting. 10. The fire burned the house to the ground. 11. I will wire you as soon as I arrive. 12. We came home in the automobile on a punctured tire. 13. I will meet you at four o'clock. 14. The more we know, the more we want to know. 15. His enthusiasm wore off after a while. 16. The

surf broke with a roar on the beach. 17. I hope you are not going to have a bad sore throat. 18. Shove the boat off from the shore. 19. Do you know the lore of the birds? 20. Will you please open the door for me? 21. I gave the horse the core of the apple. 22. At what hour shall I come to see you? 23. The fox called the grapes sour because he could not reach them.

Ur—Puckered-Corners

185. The sound of *ur*, as in "turn," shows usually only the puckered-corners movement; the *u* does not show a separate movement, but is absorbed by the *r*.

Occasionally, however, only the relaxed-medium movement is seen for *ur;* this is especially common when the sound is final, as in "fur."

And occasionally also, *ur* shows both the relaxed-medium (for the *u*) and the puckered-corners (for the *r*); this is common where the *ur* sound is followed by a vowel in another syllable, as in "hurry."

186. *Practise Words*

fur	were²	chirp	curve
firm¹	whir²	learn	yearn
verb¹	worm	turn²	hurt⁴
burr	surf	dirt³	heard⁴

187. *Sentences*

1. The muff is made of the fur of the blue fox. 2. They took a firm stand in the matter. 3. Have you ever read "The Opening of a Chestnut Burr?" 4. I hear the whir of machinery. 5. The worm will turn. 6. Let's go swimming in the surf! 7. The birds chirp happily among the trees. 8. Will you never learn any better? 9. Things will take a turn. 10. The train came around the curve. 11. Did you hurt yourself very much? 12. I never heard of that before.

———

Variant Sounds

Short ŏ

188. For the sound of short ŏ, as in "odd," "on," etc., there are two possibilities, depending upon the speaker's pronunciation.

First.—Short ŏ is more commonly heard as an extreme short sound of Italian *a* (ah); when so pronounced it shows the relaxed-wide.

Second.—Short ŏ is also quite commonly heard as an extreme short sound of broad *a* (aw); when so pronounced it shows the puckered-wide movement. A few words, such as "dog," "long," "lost," etc., are almost always heard with this sound.

189.   *Practise Words*

fop[1]	shop[2]	yacht	loft
fob[1]	chop[2]	odd[4]	long
pot	lot	hot[4]	lost
what	dot[3]	on*	dog
rob	knot[3]	off	cross
sob	cot	soft	cost

190.   *Sentences*

1. Would you like a watch fob for a Christmas present? 2. A watched pot never boils. 3. I don't know what I am going to want.

* "On" may be homophenous with "odd" and "hot"; though through to this point, the words are usually given with relaxed-wide for the *o*, while "on" is often puckered-wide. All the words in the list after "on" usually show the puckered-wide.

4. Thieves robbed the house while we were away. 5. She sobbed as if her heart would break. 6. Did you have a chop for breakfast. 7. I bought the house and lot at a great bargain. 8. You must not forget to dot your i's. 9. I slept on a cot all the time I was in camp. 10. Would you like to go for a sail with me in my yacht? 11. There was a hot fire in the grate. 12. Come on with me. 13. I'm going off for an all day tramp. 14. The turf was very soft after the long rain. 15. We had a merry time in the hay loft. 16. That is the long and short of the whole matter. 17. I thought you were lost! 18. Old Mother Hubbard went to the cupboard to fetch her poor dog a bone. 19. She was as cross as two sticks when I spoke to her. 20. What would it cost to paint the house?

Long or Short oo

191. There are a number of words, such as "roof," that are currently pronounced with either the long or the short sound of *oo*, and hence show either the puckered-narrow or the puckered-medium movement. The long sound is more common and is preferred by orthoepists.

192.   *Practise Words*

roof	soon	hoof
room	soot	hoop
root		

193.   *Sentences*

1. The roof has a bad leak. 2. There was a crowd of people in the room. 3. That is the root of the whole trouble. 4. I will be with you very soon. 5. The chimney was fairly choked with soot. 6. I saw the imprint of a deer's hoof in the woods. 7. The little girl was rolling a hoop along the walk.

A in Path

194. There are a number of words, such as "path," in which the *a* commonly has the short sound, as in "pat," and the extended-wide movement, though a somewhat broader sound, nearly equivalent to *ah*, showing the relaxed-wide movement, is more correct.

195. *Practise Words*

fast[1]	path[2]	blast	ask
vast[1]	bath[2]	class[3]	task
past	last	glass[3]	grasp

196. *Sentences*

1. I took the fast train for Boston. 2. "Let the dead past bury its dead." 3. I made a gravel path around the garden. 4. Where were you last night? 5. The house shook from the blast. 6. Would you like a glass of water? 7. I shall have to ask you to go to the post office for me. 8. When you have finished your task, you can rest for awhile. 9. A drowning man grasps at a straw.

---

x

197. The letter *x* represents a combination of two sounds, namely, of *k* and *s* (as "box"= "boks"), or of *g* and *z* (as "exact"="egzact") Hence, theoretically, the sounds represented by *x* show a combination of the throat movement and the tremor-at-corners movement; practically, however, the throat movement is seldom seen, so that *x* looks like *s* or *z*. This will be seen by contrasting "next" and "nest," "hoax," and "hoes."

198.   *Practise Words*

fox	flax	next[1]	vex
box	six	text[1]	phlox

199.   *Sentences*

1. Did you ever go on a fox hunt? 2. I bought a box of candy. 3. Her hair is the color of flax. 4. The clock has just struck six. 5. I will see you again next week. 6. I wish you would not vex the cat. 7. I have a bed of phlox in my garden.

Unaccented Vowels

200. Accented vowels are those occurring in syllables which are stressed or emphasized; unaccented vowels are those occurring in syllables which are not stressed. For example, in "after," the first syllable is stressed or accented, while the final syllable is unstressed or unaccented.

In ordinary, colloquial speech, almost all unaccented vowels are spoken very carelessly, often slovenly. The result is that they usually show either the relaxed-medium or the relaxed-narrow movement. The relaxed-medium movement is more common, and any unaccented vowel may show it; though the tendency for the vowels which (except short ă) in accented syllables would be extended, and for short ĭ, is to show the relaxed-narrow. Even these, however, may show the relaxed-medium, according to the speaker.

Many unemphatic words of one syllable have the effect of loss of accent when pronounced rapidly and naturally in sentences. Such words are particularly prepositions, as *to, of, on, by*, etc.; conjunctions, as *and, or;* the articles *a, an, the;* and auxiliary verbs, as *has, had, can*, etc.

Extended Movements, Tending, when Unaccented, to Become Relaxed–Narrow

201. The accented and unaccented vowels occurring in this group may be represented by the words: *reef, refer; fierce, ferocious; get, target; face, surface; tare, elementary.*

202. *Practise Words*

befall	depend	surface
below	erect	average
refer	eruption	yesterday
prefer	ferocious	elementary
remove	market	elementary
reward	target	rudimentary
severe	contented	rosary

203. *Sentences*

1. I will come to see you if it should befall me to be in town. 2. I went below when the weather was rough. 3. Can you refer me to a good dentist in the city? 4. I prefer not to talk about the matter. 5. I would like to have the rubbish removed from the cellar. 6. The reward of perseverance is sure. 7. There was a severe wind storm last night. 8. I depend upon you to write me all the news. 9. They are going to erect a twelve story building on the site. 10. The baby has an eruption all over his body. 11. The hunter shot the ferocious mother bear whose cubs he had captured. 12. Are you going to market this morning? 13. The marksman hit the target in the bullseye. 14. She is perfectly

contented with her lot in life. 15. The surface of the lake is frozen. 16. What is the average attendance at your church? 17. I met your friend yesterday on the street. 18. She has only an elementary education. 19. Our knowledge of electricity is still rudimentary. 20. She wore the rosary around her neck.

Relaxed Movements, Tending, when Unaccented, to Become Relaxed–Narrow

204. The accented and unaccented vowels occurring in this group may be represented by the words: p*i*t, pulp*i*t; d*i*re, d*i*rect.

205. *Practise Words*

*i*mpose	d*i*spose	hurr*y*	worm*y*
*i*nfer	p*i*ano	furr*y*	gigantic
*i*nsure	pulp*i*t	worr*y*	d*i*rect
*i*llegible	splend*i*d	wear*y*	em*i*gration

206. *Sentences*

1. Don't allow anyone to impose on you.
2. What am I to infer from her actions?
3. Have you insured the house against fire?

4. His handwriting is so illegible I cannot make out what he is trying to say. 5. I am not disposed to do anything for her. 6. I will accompany you on the piano if you will sing for us. 7. Who occupied the pulpit at church this morning? 8. We had a splendid vacation in the mountains. 9. You will miss the train unless you hurry. 10. I saw some furry animal in the woods this morning. 11. Don't worry about that. 12. I am weary of hearing him talk about his troubles. 13. I think that is a wormy nut you have. 14. Some of the trees in California are gigantic in size. 15. Can you direct me to the church I wish to find? 16. The emigration from Italy to America is very large.

————

Puckered Movements, Tending, when Unaccented to Become Relaxed–Medium

207. The accented and unaccented vowels occurring in this group may be represented by the words: t*oo*, today; acc*u*se, acc*u*sation; c*u*re, acc*u*rate; f*u*ll, awful; s*u*re, erasure; *o*pe, *o*pinion; *o*re, *o*ration; *awe*, *au*gust (adj.); *o*ff, *o*fficial; s*ir*, s*u*rprise. In rapid speech, these unaccented vowels tend to become relaxed, though in more careful speech, they will show a slight puckering of the lips.

208. *Practise Words*

today	wonderful	august
tomorrow	delightful	authentic
rubescent	wilful	authority
superior	pleasure	official
stupendous	measure	offensive
accusation	feature	forlorn
commutation	opinion	mirror
accurate	propose	rumor
funereal	violin	river
awful	oration	surprise
beautiful	horizon	

209. *Sentences*

1. Are you going to town today or tomorrow? 2. The rubescent moon rose over the hills. 3. Means of transportation today are much superior to those of a century ago. 4. There has been stupendous progress in all lines of invention. 5. I do not believe the accusation against him is true. 6. He gave a very accurate report of what he saw.

7. The sunset last night was more than beautiful.   8. That opera singer has a wonderful voice.   9. The weather was most delightful all the time we were gone.   10. It will give me a great deal of pleasure to have you go with me. 11. Will you measure me and see how tall I am?   12. What is your opinion of the story? 13. I do not propose to allow him to have the book.   14. Do you play the violin?   15. There was not a single ship on the horizon.   16. Who is your authority for the statement?   17. I have the official report of the association. 18. You look very forlorn this afternoon. 19. The lake was like a mirror this morning early.   20. I heard a rumor that you were going to move out west.   21. Will you row me across the river?   22. Were you very much surprised to find me here?

Relaxed Movements, Tending, when Unaccented, to Become Relaxed–Medium

210. The accented and unaccented vowels occurring in this group may be represented by the words: *up, upon*; *far, sofa*; *con, convince*.

211. *Practise Words*

upon	precious	parade
until	illustrious	barometer
suppose	spontaneous	confer
succeed	sofa	confession
suggestion	drama	commission
sufficient	gorilla	objection
discus	papa	oppose
luscious	papa	occur

212. *Sentences*

1. Upon my word, I never thought of that. 2. I will wait here until the sun goes down. 3. What do you suppose they will say when they hear the news? 4. If you would succeed, you must persist. 5. Have you any suggestions to make for the party? 6. There will be sufficient time to finish everything. 7. That was a luscious peach I had for lunch. 8. She lost two of the precious stones from her ring. 9. Longfellow was the most illustrious of our American poets. 10. The fire was caused by spontaneous combustion. 11. Both of them sat on the sofa together. 12. I saw a gorilla at the menagerie yesterday. 13. The little boy kissed his papa good-bye. 14. All the

children ran to see the circus parade. 15. The barometer fell very low last night. 16. We must confer as to the best course to pursue. 17. Honest confession is good for the soul. 18. Have you any objection to my going with you? 19. I shall not oppose your going if you wish to. 20. I hope you will not let that occur again.

Extended Movements, Tending, when Un-accented, to Become Relaxed–Medium

213. The accented and unaccented vowels occurring in this group may be represented by the words: *able, ability; add, advance.*

214.　　*Practise Words*

ability	facility	affirm	workman
above	casino	appear	musical
about	advance	again	distant

215.　　*Sentences*

1. She has a great deal of literary ability.
2. The new house is just beginning to show

above ground. 3. I will meet you at the office at about twelve o'clock. 4. Have you any facility with carpenter's tools? 5. I should like to have you go with me to the casino to-night. 6. You are advancing very rapidly in your work. 7. I will affirm the truth of the statement positively. 8. You appear to be having a good deal of trouble. 9. All the King's horses and all the King's men couldn't put Humpty Dumpty together again. 10. The man who helped me was a very good work-man. 11. Have you any musical talent? 12. How far is the moon distant from the earth?

Lost Unaccented Vowels

216. There are some words in which the unaccented vowel is either lost or so slightly pronounced as to show no movement, as "poison" becomes "pois'n."

217.   *Practise Words*

poison	pleasant	mission	nation
lesson	fasten	ocean	legion

218. *Sentences*

1. The bottle was marked "poison." 2. I hope that will be a lesson to you. 3. We had very pleasant weather for the journey. 4. Will you help me fasten my skates on? 5. Have you any special mission in going to Chicago? 6. "My bonnie lies over the ocean." 7. "The fate of a nation was riding that night." 8. There was a legion of flies in the house.

SECOND OUTLINE OF DAILY PRACTISE, THROUGH SECTION VI

This work consists of practise from material given in Sections I, IV, V and VI. The *review* and the *lesson for the day* from each section as practised with assistant may be taken consecutively if desired. For such practise, given an hour for the work, divide the time approximately as follows:

From Section I. . . . . .20 minutes
From Section IV. . . . . . . .15 minutes
From Section V. . . . . .10 minutes
From Section VI. . . . . . . .15 minutes

This limit of time is not intended to be inflexible; modifications according to the pupil will often have to be made. But as a rule I find it unwise to spend more than 15 consecutive minutes on any work from Section IV.

A. Review with assistant (all review practise should be rapid).
  I. From Section I.
    a. *The Story.* Same as in first outline, p. 94.

II. From Section IV.

a. *Exercises.* Follow specific directions for review given under each exercise.

III. From Section V.

a. *Colloquial Sentences* and *Forms.* The *sentences* should be reviewed as read rapidly and skipping around. The *forms* should be reviewed for the special form indicated, the assistant following the method described for mirror practise.

IV. From Section VI.

a. *Homophenous Words.* These should be reviewed in the same manner as previously practised in the *lesson for the day.*

B. Lesson for the Day.

I. From Section I.

a. *The Story.* Follow same method as directed in first outline, p. 95, except that in the skipping around practise, two or even three stories should be used, skipping back and forth from one to the other. See also advice under C in first outline, p. 99.

II. From Section IV.
  a. *Exercises.* Follow specific directions given under each exercise.

III. From Section V.
  a. *Colloquial Sentences* and *Forms.* Take from ten to twenty *sentences* for a lesson. Do not take up the *forms* until the *sentences* and *proverbs* have been completed. Take one *form,* with all sentences written or suggested thereunder, for a lesson.

IV. From Section VI.
  a. *Homophenous Words.* Practise as directed.

V. Conversation Practise. See Chapter IV.

VI. From Sections I, IV and V.
  a. *Mirror practise* should follow and supplement the work under these sections done with assistant. Directions for each are given in their proper places.

C. Preparation for the New Lesson.
  I. From Section I.
    a. *The Story.* See first outline under C, p. 99.

II. FROM SECTION IV.

   a. *Exercises.* Mirror practise as directed.

III. FROM SECTION V.

   a. *Colloquial Sentences* and *Forms.* The *sentences* and *proverbs* should not be practised or even read. The *forms* should be practised with mirror as directed.

IV. FROM SECTION VI.

   a. *Homophenous Words.* The preliminary preparation for the pupil, before practise with assistant, is described under this section, see p. 304.

SECTION IV

EXERCISES

219. The exercises in this section of the work are intended for eye training; they therefore provide particularly good material for mirror practise. The pupil and the assistant must observe always the caution to speak naturally, without undue emphasis, and as rapidly as the pupil's skill permits. Fifteen minutes is usually enough to spend at one time on such eye training as this section gives.

Vowel Exercises

220. Chapter VII gives the classification of the vowel movements. Vowels, it will be remembered, are divided into three groups, the *puckered*, the *relaxed*, and the *extended*. Under each group we have a *narrow* opening between the lips, a *medium* opening, and a *wide* opening. The following table groups the vowel sounds according to these classes;

diphthongs are given in parenthesis under that classification to which their radical element belongs.

	Puckered	*Relaxed*	*Extended*
Narrow	o͞o (ū)	ĭ	ē
Medium	o͝o	ŭ	ĕ (ä)
Wide	aw (ō, oy)	ah (ow, ī) ă	

It will facilitate the correct pronunciation of these vowel sounds, and hence their proper study, if they are incorporated in words, as follows:

	Puckered	*Relaxed*	*Extended*
Narrow	coon	kid	keen
Medium	good	cut	get
Wide	cawed	cart	cat

The first step in the study of these words is for the pupil to try them on his own mouth, watching in the mirror the formation of the vowels. Compare the formation on the lips with the description given. When you have satisfied yourself that you can see the indicated characteristics of each vowel movement (never mind the consonants for the present), then proceed as follows: Pronounce the three words of the puckered group one after the other, and watch on your own lips in the mirror the difference between the narrow, the medium, and the wide openings between the upper and lower lips. Speak the words rather quickly and without any undue emphasis or exaggeration. Then say the same words again in reverse order, then in several different orders, over and over, until you feel that you have mastered theoretically at least the peculiarities of the puckered vowels. Then try the words of the relaxed group, and then those of the extended group in the same manner.

Now take the three words in the narrow group, "coon, kid, keen," and watching your mouth in the mirror, observe the difference between the puckered movement, the relaxed, and the extended. Say the same words again in reverse order, then in several different orders, over and over, until you feel that you have mastered the differences between the narrow vowels. Then try the words of the medium group, and then those of the wide group similarly.

Your method of practising these words with an assistant is in part like to the method of practising them with the mirror. That is, let your assistant read to you, three at a time, the words of the puckered group, over and over, in many different orders, while you repeat the words after him. Then practise the relaxed group, then the extended, then the narrow, then the medium, and then the wide, in the same way. In all of this practise your assistant should speak fairly rapidly, inaudibly, and should go over the words repeatedly until you have mastered them. When you have truly mastered the words in their groups, then your assistant should practise with you three words at a time, skipping around from group to group, until you can get all readily and quickly in this way.

You will not accomplish such mastery in one day or ten. But by keeping at it you ought to be able in time to be sure of all the vowels except short ĭ, which is the hardest of them all, and perhaps also long ē and short ĕ.

The vowels in the exercises below are combined, both after and before, with all the fundamental consonant movements. Practise as directed above, taking one or two complete groups, as indicated by the numbers, for a lesson. The review work on these exercises, from lesson to lesson, should consist chiefly of the practise with assistant cf three words at a time, skipping around from group to group, the pupil repeating. As proficiency is gained, four and then five words at a time may be practised in this way.

(1)	boot	bit	beet	hōōp	hip	heap
	book	but	bet	hŏŏp (?)	up	ebb
	pawn	bard	bat	orb	arm	am

(2)	food	fit	feet	hōōf	if	eve
	foot	fun	fed	hŏŏf (?)	huff	deaf
	fawn	far	fat	cough	carve	have

(3)		you	yin	ye
		———	young	yet
		yaw	yarn	yak

(4)	coon	kid	keen	duke	ink	eke
	good	cut	get	cook	hug	egg
	cawed	cart	cat	auk	ark	hag

(5)	toot	tin	tea	hoot	it	eat
	took	tuck	ten	hood	hut	end
	dawn	tar	tan	awed	art	add

(6)

loot	lit	lean	cool	ill	eel
look	luck	let	pull	hull	ell
lawn	lard	lad	awl	Carl	Hal

(7)

thew	thin	thee	tooth	kith	teeth
——	thug	then	——	doth	death
thaw	thar	that	north	hearth	hath

(8)

zoo	sit	seat	ooze	is	ease
sook	sun	set	puss	us	guess
saw	sard	sat	awes	cars	as

(9)

rue	rid	reed
rook	run	red
raw	rah	rat

(10)

wooed	wit	weed
wood	won	wet
wart	what	whack

(11)

shoot	shin	sheet	douche	itch	each
should	shun	shed	push	hush	edge
short	shard	shad	torch	harsh	ash

Consonant Exercises

221. In the following exercise material is given for the study of the consonant movements before vowels:

> back, fag, whack; fag, whack, rack; whack, rack, sack; rack, sack, shack; sack, shack, thank; shack, thank, lack; thank, lack, tack; lack, tack, yak; tack, yak, gag.

Study these words with the mirror, in the following manner: Take the three words of the first group, "back, fag, whack." Observe closely the differences, which you will notice lie solely in the initial consonants, the *b*, *f*, and *wh*. Repeat the words in direct order, reverse order, and several different orders, until these consonant movements are thoroughly learned. Then practise the next group of three, "fag, whack, rack," in the same way; and so on with each group.

You will then be ready to try them with your assistant; the method for doing so is similar to the method for mirror practise; that is, the assistant should read to you the three words of a group, going over and over them, each time changing the order, until you can repeat them readily and quickly. Then try three words skipping around, changing them from different groups.

It is important, both in mirror practise and in practise with assistant, that the words of a group should not be pronounced slowly, word by word, but rapidly, the three words together.

The words of the first five groups can be learned perfectly. The real difficulty will begin with the introduction of l in the sixth group. The seventh, eighth, and ninth groups are all hard and cannot be learned with absolute perfection. The ninth group particularly is so hard as to make impossible any high degree of accuracy; for these consonants are the ones that must frequently be told by the context.

Complete material for these consonant exercises is given below, using the eleven fundamental consonant movements in combination with the nine fundamental vowel movements, both as initial and as final elements; consonants w and y are never final sounds, and final r is usually so slurred as to show no movement, and so w, y, and r are omitted as final elements in the following exercises. Practise as above, taking two to four complete groups, as indicated by the numbers, for a lesson. The review work on these exercises, from lesson to lesson, should consist chiefly of the practise with assistant of three words at a time, skipping around from group to group, the pupil repeating. As proficiency is gained, four and then five words at a time may be practised in this way.

(1)   back, fag, whack;   fag, whack, rack; whack, rack, sack;   rack, sack, shack; sack, shack, thank;   shack, thank, lack; thank, lack, tack;   lack, tack, yak; tack, yak, gag.

(2)   am, have, has;   have, has, hash;   has, hash, hath;   hash, hath, Hal;   hath, Hal, hat;   Hal, hat, hag.

(3)   bard, far, what;   far, what, rah;   what, rah, sard;   rah, sard, shard;   sard, shard, thar;   shard, thar, lard;   thar, lard, tart; lard, tart, yard;   tart, yard, card.

(4)   arm, carve, cars;   carve, cars, harsh; cars, harsh, hearth;   harsh, hearth, Carl; hearth, Carl, art;   Carl, art, ark.

(5) paw, for, war; for, war, raw; war, raw,
saw; raw, saw, short; saw, short, thaw;
short, thaw, law; thaw, law, daw; law,
daw, yawn; daw, yawn, caw.

(6) orb, cough, awes; cough, awes, torch;
awes, torch, north; torch, north, all;
north, all, awed; all, awed, auk.

(7) bet, fed, wet; fed, wet, red; wet, red,
set; red, set, shed; set, shed, then;
shed, then, let; then, let, ten; let, ten,
yet; ten, yet, get.

(8) ebb, deaf, guess; deaf, guess, edge;
guess, edge, death; edge, death, ell;
death, ell, end; ell, end, egg.

(9) pun, fun, won; fun, won, run; won,
run, sun; run, sun, shun; sun, shun,
thug; shun, thug, luck; thug, luck,
tuck; luck, tuck, young; tuck, young,
cut.

10) up, huff, us; huff, us, hush; us, hush,
doth; hush, doth, hull; doth, hull,
hut; hull, hut, hug.

(11) book, foot, wood; foot, wood, rook;
wood, rook, sook; rook, sook, shook;
sook, shook, look; shook, look, took;
look, took, cook.

(12) (hoŏp, hoŏf)*; puss, push, pull; push,
pull, put; pull, put, book.

(13) bee, fee, wee; fee, wee, reed; wee,
reed, see; reed, see, she; see, she,
thee; she, thee, lee; thee, lee, tea;
lee, tea, ye; tea, ye, key.

(14) heap, eve, ease; eve, ease, each; ease,
each, teeth; each, teeth, eel; teeth,
eel, eat; eel, eat, eke.

(15) bit, fit, wit; fit, wit, rid; wit, rid, sit;
rid, sit, shin; sit, shin, thin; shin, thin,
lit; thin, lit, tin; lit, tin, yin; tin,
yin, kin.

(16) hip, if, is; if, is, itch; is, itch, kith;
itch, kith, ill; kith, ill, it; ill, it, ink.

---

* The vowel in this group is commonly long o͞o, but sometimes
is heard as short o͝o.

(17) boot, food, wooed; food, wooed, rued;
wooed, rued, sued; rued, sued, shoot;
sued, shoot, thew; shoot, thew, loot;
thew, loot, toot; loot, toot, you; toot,
you, coot.

(18) hōop, hōof, ooze; hōof, ooze, douche;
ooze, douche, tooth; douche, tooth, tool;
tooth, tool, toot; tool, toot, duke.

Double Consonant Exercises

222. The object of the following exercises
is drill in observing the use or omission of
certain more difficult consonants when combined with other consonants. In the first
exercises, for example, the student watches
for the use or omission of *r* (puckered-corners)
in the couplets "three, thee," etc. Practise
them before the mirror, taking only the two
words of a couplet at a time, and observing
the movement for the *r*. Practise them with
your assistant, by couplets, each couplet
being given several times in direct and reverse
order, while you concentrate your attention
on the puckered-corners movement for the *r*.

To facilitate your doing this, practise in these two ways: *First*, do not try to see the vowels at all; simply watch for the *r*, and tell your assistant whether you see it in the first or second word. *Second*, repeat the couplets after your assistant as he reads them to you.

In reviewing these exercises with your assistant, have them given to you thus: "thee, three, thee," "three, thee, thee," "thee, three, three," etc. You should repeat them.

223. To watch for *r:*

(1) three, thee; thray, they; thrash, than; thrill, thill; thrum, thumb; thrive, thy; through, thew; thraw, thaw.

(2) cree, key; gray, gay; crap, cap; crick, kick; crumb, cup; cry, guy; crew, coo; crook, cook; craw, caw.

(3) tree, tee; dray, day; track, tack; trick, tick; truck, tuck; try, tie; true too; draw, daw.

(4) free, fee; fray, fay; frank, fag; frill, fill; front, fun; fry, fie; fruit, food; fraw, faw.

(5) bree, bee; bray, bay; brat, bat; prick, pick; brung, bug; pry, pie; brew, boo; brook, book; braw, paw.

(6) shree, she; shray, shay; shrank, shank; shrimp, ship; shrug, shuck; shrine, shy; shrew, shoe; shraw, shaw.

224. To watch for *l*:

(1) glee, key; clay, gay; clap, cap, click, kick; club, cub; glide, guy; clue, coo; claw, caw.

(2) flee, fee; flay, fay; flag, fag; flip, fib; flush, fudge; fly, fie; flew, foo; flaw, faw.

(3) plea, pea; play, pay; black, back; blink, big; plug, pug; ply, pie; blew, boo; plaw, paw.

(4) slee, see; slay, say; slag, sag; slick, sick; slung, sung; sly, sigh; slew, soo; slaw, saw.

225. To watch for *s*:

(1) skee, key; scay, gay; scat, cat; skit, kit; scum, cup; sky, guy; scoo, coo· scaw, caw.

(2) spee, pea; spay, pay; spat, pat; spit, pit; spunk, punk; spy, pie; spoo, poo; spaw, paw.

(3) swee, we; sway, way; swag, whack; swig, wig; swung, won; swine, why; swoo, woo; swaw, waw.

(4) slee, lee; slay, lay; slag, lag; slick, lick; slug, luck; sly, lie; sloo, loo; slaw, law.

(5) stee, tee; stay, day; stack, tack; stick, tick; stuck, tuck; sty, tie; stoo, too; stood, took; staw, daw.

226. To watch for *t* (or *d*):

(1) tree, ree; tray, ray; track, rack; trick, rick; truck, rug; try, rye; true, rue; draw, raw.

(2) stee, see; stay, say; stack, sack; sting, sing; stung, sung; sty, sigh; stoo, soo; stood, sook; staw, saw.

227. To watch for *k* (or hard *c*, or hard *g*):

(1) cree, ree; cray, ray; crag, rag; crick, rick; crumb, rum; cry, rye; crew, rue; crook, rook; craw, raw.

(2) skee, see; scay, say; scat, sat; skit, sit; scum, sum; sky, sigh; scoo, soo; scaw, saw.

(3) glee, lee; clay, lay; clack, lack; click, lick; cluck, luck; glide, lie; clue, loo; claw, law.

DOUBLE CONSONANT CONTRAST EXERCISES

228. The object of the following exercises is to watch for the change, in double consonants, from one consonant movement to another. Practise them before the mirror, taking them by couplets, and contrasting the movements for the indicated sounds. Also practise them with an assistant.

In practising with an assistant, the pupil concentrates first on the movement for one of the contrasted sounds, then on the other, and then on both. For example, in the first exercise, the pupil concentrates on the movement for *r* and tells whether it occurs in the first or second word of the couplet; then he concentrates similarly for *l;* then he repeats the couplets.

Review by triplets with assistant in the manner directed in paragraph 222.

229. To watch for the change from *r* to *l:*

(1)   bree, plea; pray, play; prank, plank; brink, blink; brung, plug; pry, ply; brew, blew; braw, plaw.

(2)   free, flee; fray, flay; frank, flank; frill, flit; front, flunk; fry, fly; froo, flew; fraw, flaw.

(3)   cree, glee; cray, clay; crank, clank; crick, click; crumb, club; cry, glide; crew, clue; craw, claw.

230. To watch for the change from *s* to *k* (or hard *c*, or hard *g*):

(1)   slee, glee; slay, clay; slack, clank; slick, click; slung, clung; sly, glide; slew, clew; slaw, claw.

To watch for the change from *t* to *l:*

(2)   stee, slee; stay, slay; stag, slag; stick, slick; stung, slung; sty, sly; stoo, sloo; staw, slaw.

231. To watch for the change from *t* (or *d*) to *k* (or hard *c* or hard *g*):

(1) tree, cree; tray, cray; track, crack; trick, crick; trump, crumb; try, cry; true, crew; draw, craw.

(2) stee, skee; stay, scay; stab, scab; still, skill; stuck, skunk; sty, sky; stoo, scoo; staw, scaw.

VOWEL EXERCISES IN SENTENCES

232. The object of the following exercises is drill with those vowel sounds most likely to be confused. In the order of the similarity of their movements, the sounds are: *aw*, as in "awl," (puckered-wide); *ur*, as in "turn," (puckered-corners); *ŏŏ*, as in "hook," (puckered-medium); *ŭ*, as in "hut," (relaxed-medium); *ĭ*, as in "hit," (relaxed-narrow); *ē*, as in "he," (extended-narrow); *ĕ*, as in "bet," (extended-medium); *ā*, as in "ale," (extended-medium—relaxed-narrow); *ă*, as in "bat," (extended-wide); and *ī*, as in "high," (relaxed-wide—relaxed-narrow). Short *ĕ* and long $\bar{a}$ are practically the same in rapid speech; though in slower speech a difference may be seen. See paragraph 162. Words have been chosen in which the movements for these sounds are the only movements changed; occasionally it has been necessary to use manufactured words with phonetic spelling; and occasionally, too, obscure consonants, such as t and k, have been used interchangeably in the same groups. These words have been put in a sentence, the sentence remaining unchanged throughout each exercise except for the one change of movement in the chosen word.

In practising these exercises before the mirror, always pronounce the whole sentence, but concentrate attention on the particular vowel movement indicated.

In practising with an assistant, he reads the sentences, rapidly and naturally, while the pupil repeats them. Have each exercise read first in order, and then repeated promiscuously a number of times until well mastered. The words should always be given *in their sentences*, and never alone by themselves. The review with the assistant should be done in the same manner.

(1) The auk is large.　(2) The pawn is black.
　" irk " "　　　" burn " "
　" hook " "　　　" put " "
　" hug " "　　　" bun " "
　" ink " "　　　" bin " "
　" eke " "　　　" bean " "
　" egg " "　　　" pen " "
　" ache " "　　　" pane " "
　" hag " "　　　" pan " "
　" Ike " "　　　" pine " "

(3) The fawn is pretty.　(4) My yawn is deep.
　" fern " "　　　" yearn " "
　" foot " "　　　" young " "
　" fun " "　　　" yin " "
　" fin " "　　　" yeen " "
　" feat " "　　　" yet " "
　" fen " "　　　" yane " "
　" fane " "　　　" yak " "
　" fan " "　　　" yarn " "
　" fine " "

(5) I caught ten fish. (6) The talk of the town.
   " curt   "   "   " dirk " "   "
   " cook   "   "   " took " "   "
   " cut   "   "   " tuck " "   "
   " kid   "   "   " tick " "   "
   " keen   "   "   " teak " "   "
   " get   "   "   " deck " "   "
   " gain   "   "   " take " "   "
   " cat   "   "   " tack " "   "
   " kite   "   "   " dike " "   "

(7) The lawn is wet. (8) Your thought is good.
   " learn " "   " third   "   "
   " look " "   " thud   "   "
   " luck " "   " thin   "   "
   " lit " "   " theen   "   "
   " leed " "   " then   "   "
   " let " "   " thane   "   "
   " lane " "   " than   "   "
   " lad " "   " thine   "   "
   " line " "

(9) He sawed the wood. (10) He wrought it well.

" surd " "   " rook " "
" sook " "   " rut " "
" sun " "   " rid " "
" sit " "   " reed " "
" seat " "   " red " "
" set " "   " rate " "
" sate " "   " rat " "
" sat " "   " rite " "
" site " "

(11) The walk is hard. (12) He jawed the man.

" word " "   " shirt " "
" wood " "   " should " "
" won " "   " shun " "
" wit " "   " shin " "
" weed " "   " sheen " "
" wet " "   " shed " "
" wait " "   " shade " "
" wag " "   " shad " "
" wide " "   " shied " "

CONSONANT EXERCISES IN SENTENCES

233. The object of the following exercises is drill with those consonant sounds most likely to be confused. In the order of the similarity of their movements, the sounds are: *r* (puckered-corners); *l* (pointed-tongue-to-gum); *t*, *d*, *n* (flat-tongue-to-gum); *s*, *z* (tremor-at-corners); *y* (relaxed-narrow); and *k*, *g*, *ng* (throat movement). The practise should be with the mirror, and with an assistant, as directed in paragraph 232, except that these exercises are drills with consonants, while the former were drills with vowels. The consonants are given first as the initial elements in the words chosen. Remember that the words should always be given *in their sentences*, and never alone by themselves.

These exercises should be developed further by the assistant for the other and easier consonants, as *p* (*b*, *m*), *f* (*v*), *w* (*wh*), *sh* (*ch*, *j*), *th*. For example, in the first exercise, use, in the sentence, these words also: *back*, *fag*, *whack*, *shack*, *thank*. In the second exercise, use also: *bite*, *fight*, *white*, *shied*, *thine*. And so on for the other exercises.

(1) The rack is strong.
    " lack " "
    " tack " "
    " sack " "
    " yak " "
    " gag " "

(2) The right is mine.
    " light " "
    " tight " "
    " site " "
    " kite " "

(3) Cook the raw meat.
    " " law "
    " " daw "
    " " saw "
    " " yaw "
    " " caw "

(4) The ray is bright.
    " lay " "
    " day " "
    " say " "
    " yea " "
    " gay " "

(5) The rung is broken.
    " lung " "
    " tongue " "
    " sung " "
    " young " "
    " gun " "

(6) The rook is black.
    " look " "
    " took " "
    " sook " "
    " cook " "

(7) A ream is enough.
    " leap " "
    " team " "
    " seam " "
    " yeep " "
    " keep " "

(8) The rick is old.
    " lick " "
    " tick " "
    " sick " "
    " kick " "

(9) The route is long.
     "   loot   "   "
     "   toot   "   "
     "   suit   "   "
     "   coot   "   "

---

234. The consonants are given below as the *final* elements in the words chosen. Practise as with the exercises in paragraph **233.**

Develop these exercises by practising too for final *p* (*b, m*), *f* (*v*), *sh* (*ch, j*), *th*. E. g., in the first exercise use also: *gap, gaff, gash, gath.* And so on for the other exercises.

(1) The gal has come.   (2) The tile was broken.
     "   cat   "   "   "   tide   "   "
     "   gas   "   "   "   dice   "   "
     "   gag   "   "   "   dike   "   "

(3) The marl is valuable.   (4) The doll is pretty.
     "   mart   "   "   "   dot   "   "
     "   mars   "   "   "   dock "   "
     "   mark   "   "

(5) The pall   is heavy. (6) The bell is loud.
   "   pawn "   "   "   bet "   "
   "   pause "   "   "   Bess "   "
   "   balk "   "   "   peck "   "

(7) The mull is warm. (8) The pull is strong.
   "   mud "   "   "   put   "   "
   "   muss "   "   "   puss "   "
   "   mug "   "   "   book "   "

(9) The meal is ready. (10) The mill is small.
   "   beet "   "   "   mitt "   "
   "   peace "   "   "   miss "   "
   "   peak "   "   "   pick "   "

(11) The tool   is sharp.
      "   toot "   "
      "   noose "   "
      "   dook "   "

Prefix Exercises

235. The object of the following exercises is a study of certain prefixes which are commonly confused. Practise with the mirror; also with an assistant. In either case, the whole sentence should always be pronounced; but you should concentrate your attention on the prefix indicated. Review in same way.

(1) You may emend the statement.
"   "   depend "   "

The effect was momentous.
" defect "   "

The more erect, the better.
"   "   direct, "   "

He'll be exposed tomorrow.
"   "   disposed   "

He was ejected with cause.
"   "   dejected "   "

The election is over.
" delection "   "

How inane the book.
"   detain "   "

The egression was large.
" digression "   "

(2) I've amended   the resolution.
   " commended "   "

We will affirm our opinion.
   " " confirm "   "

I have a relative in Dover.
   " " correlative "   "

We gave assent to the scheme.
   " " consent "   "   "

Our house will adjoin yours.
   " " " conjoin   "

Make no allusion to the matter.
   " " collusion "   "   "

That will attain our desires.
   " " contain "   "

Let it not occur again.
   " " " concur "

(3) Don't reprove the students.
   " we prove "   "

Don't revere him too much.
   " we fear "   "   "

Don't resign the office.
   " we sign "   "

Don't record that vote.
  "   we cord   "   "

Do relieve him tomorrow.
  " we leave "   "

Do retain a lawyer.
  " we deign   "

Do rejoin our party in Paris.
  " we join "   "   "   "

EXERCISES WITH VERB ENDINGS

236. The object of the following exercises is a study of the verb endings that are commonly confused. Practise as directed in paragraph 235.

(1) The dog treed the coon.
  "   " treeing "   "
  "   " trees   "   "

He rapped on the door.
  " rapping "   "   "
  " raps   "   "   "

She vowed vengeance.
  " vowing   "
  " vows   "

The man hurried home.
"   "   hurrying "
"   "   hurries   "

He lied to me.
" lying " "
" lies   " "

The man received the letter.
"   "   receiving "   "
"   "   receives   "   "

The woman rued her mistake.
"   "   ruing "   "
"   "   rues "   "

The dust blurred my sight.
"   "   blurring "   "
"   "   blurs   "   "

The traveler viewed the river.
"   "   viewing "   "
"   "   views   "   "

He bathed in the ocean.
" bathing " "   "
" bathes " "   "

(2) The wind howled in the trees.
    "   " howling " "   "
    "   " howls   " "   "

The man earned a dollar.
  "   " earning "   "
  "   " earns   "   "

He employed the laborer.
 " employing "   "
 " employs   "   "

The agent showed his goods.
  "   " showing "   "
  "   " shows   "   "

Baby weighed eleven pounds.
 " weighing   "   "
 " weighs   "   "

The lawyer doubted the witness.
  "   " doubting "   "
  "   " doubts   "   "

The sun thawed the ice.
  " " thawing " "
  " " thaws " "

Life used him well.
  "   using "   "
  "   uses   "   "

The cat watched the mouse hole.
  "   " watching "   "   "
  "   " watches   "   "   "

The boat rocked in the swell.
  "   "   rocking " "   "
  "   "   rocks   " "   "

Suffix Exercises

237. Drills with suffixes may be obtained from the material given below by putting the words in sentences. The words are given by couplets, as "rub, rubber," etc.; the drill is to observe the effect of the addition of a suffix. Remember, this work should be studied not with the words alone, but with the words in sentences, which the student may readily compose for himself. Practise with the mirror; also with an assistant.

An example will best illustrate the method of giving these exercises. Take the couplet, *rub, rubber*. Form a sentence containing *rub*, having the word occur in the middle of the

sentence, not at the beginning or end. E. g.,
"Will you rub that out?" Then use the
same sentence, only substituting *rubber* for
rub, as, "Will you rubber that out?" Repeat many times. The other couplets should
be practised similarly. The aim is of course
to see the suffix by sight and not by sense.

Review with assistant in same manner.

(1) -er—rub, rubber; love, lover; cow,
cower; poor, poorer; mice, miser;
watch, watcher; with, wither; toil,
toiler; dine, diner; quick, quicker;
pretty, prettier.

(2) -ly—home, homely; love, lovely; miser,
miserly; nice, nicely; fresh, freshly;
earth, earthly; pull, pulley; man,
manly; quick, quickly; ready, readily.

(3) -en, (-n)—damp, dampen; deaf, deafen;
care, cairn; poise, poison; fresh,
freshen; earth, earthen; fall, fallen;
bid, bidden; quick, quicken.

(4) -y—worm, wormy; huff, huffy; fur,
furry; biz, busy; fish, fishy; earth,
earthy; pearl, pearly; red, ready;
trick, tricky.

SECTION V

238. It is obviously good practise to train the eye to catch the common forms and expressions which pass from mouth to mouth again and again in a day's conversation. They may be divided into two classes, first, complete colloquial sentences, and, second, parts of sentences, forms or phrases.

The aim in studying these sentences and forms should be to memorize them; that is, to commit them to what may be called the visual memory. This is not the memory that enables us to recite what we have learned, but that which enables us infallibly to recognize by sight objects or movements studied. The diamond expert takes a handful of unmounted gems and by color or form or the slightest peculiarities instantly tells one from the other; whereas the untrained eye could not pick out one in ten. It is practise in close observation that gives the eye this quickness and sharpness in recognizing the particular object, and it is just such practise that the lip-reader requires in the study of these colloquial forms.

In studying the sentences, practise them both with the mirror and with an assistant, and go over them again and again. The mirror practise should be done according to the directions in Chapter XI; the practise with an assistant as directed in Chapter X, and this practise should preferably precede the mirror practise.

The sentences following are not a complete list; such a list would be impossible. But each of them will probably suggest one or several more, which, as directed in the chapter on Sentence Practise, should be used as well as the original sentences. Practise from ten to twenty sentences and their variations for one lesson.

Colloquial Sentences

239. 1. How do you do?   2. How are you?
3. Good morning.   4. What's your name?
5. Where do you live?   6. How is your mother? 7. Have you been ill? 8. I have a cold.
9. Which way shall I go?   10. Where are you

going? 11. What car shall I take? 12. What time does the train leave? 13. What's the matter? 14. What's up? 15. I'm tired. 16. I'm thirsty. 17. Will you get me a glass of water? 18. Never mind. 19. Don't trouble yourself. 20. Did you hear me? 21. What did you say? 22. I didn't say so. 23. What was that? 24. What do you want? 25. Is that what you want? 26. I'm not so sure of that. 27. You don't say so. 28. That's not so. 29. What will you bet? 30. Please hurry. 31. There's time enough. 32. There's time to burn. 33. What time is it? 34. I haven't time to-day. 35. I'm in a hurry. 36. How much time have you? 37. Have you time enough? 38. I'm too busy. 39. Give me time. 40. Hurry up. 41. Don't waste so much time. 42. What time can you come? 43. It's very late. 44. I must go now. 45. Don't be in a hurry. 46. Will you stay to dinner? 47. I'm going home. 48. Come again. 49. Come and see us soon. 50. Are you coming? 51. I'm not ready. 52. I'm going away. 53. May I go with you? 54. I'll be with you in a minute. 55. Be patient. 56. I'm coming. 57. We shall expect you. 58. Did you receive my letter? 59. Will you

mail my letter? 60. Has the mail come?
61. Let me know at once. 62. Will you tele-
phone? 63. May I use the 'phone? 64. What
can I do for you? 65. You are very kind.
66. Let me help you. 67. I can't do it. 68. You
might try. 69. You can do it. 70. That
will do. 71. What else could I do? 72. It's
up to you. 73. It's very tiresome. 74. It's
too hard. 75. It isn't worth while. 76. Let
me try. 77. It's no use. 78. I'll do my best.
79. There's nothing to do. 80. Let's try again.
81. I don't want to. 82. Do it now. 83. Don't
put it off. 84. It's a beautiful day. 85. It's
very warm to-day. 86. It's snowing hard.
87. It's going to rain. 88. Where will you
spend the summer? 89. Are you going abroad?
90. When do you sail? 91. Have you ever
been abroad? 92. Will you be gone long?
93. Won't you write to me? 94. Who told
you so? 95. I told you so. 96. Don't you
know? 97. I don't know. 98. I don't care.
99. What do you expect? 100. I think you're
wrong. 101. How did it happen? 102. I
know that. 103. Who's that? 104. Did you
notice that? 105. What are you doing here?
106. I think so. 107. Don't do that. 108. Let's
do it. 109. Oh, that's all right. 110. Where

have you been? 111. I thought you were lost. 112. I haven't seen you for a long time. 113. Didn't you see me? 114. I didn't see you. 115. Shall I see you to-morrow? 116. Am I in the way? 117. That's a good thing. 118. I like that. 119. How much is it? 120. Shut the window. 121. Do you feel a draught? 122. Are you warm enough? 123. The room is very warm. 124. Will you go for a walk? 125. Where shall we go? 126. Let's walk home. 127. I'm going by the subway. 128. Here we are. 129. Where are we? 130. Don't worry. 131. Don't forget. 132. I forgot all about it. 133. Don't bother me. 134. Have you read the paper? 135. What's the news? 136. I'm glad to hear it. 137. Wait a minute. 138. She's not at home. 139. Will you call again? 140. Do you know him? 141. Let me see. 142. Is that enough? 143. It's more than enough. 144. There's more to come. 145. I'm almost through. 146. I want some more. 147. Are there any more? 148. May I have one? 149. Is that all? 150. That's all.

PROVERBS

240. The following familiar proverbs may well be studied; take ten or twenty for a lesson. Have your assistant give the proverb and when understood give a variation. Another proverb may be used if it is apt. For review have your assistant read the proverbs studied in the previous lesson, skipping about quickly from one to the other.

1. A bird in the hand is worth two in the bush.
2. A drowning man grasps at a straw.
3. A fool and his money are soon parted.
4. A friend in need is a friend indeed.
5. A good beginning makes a good ending.
6. A little knowledge is a dangerous thing.
7. A miss is as good as a mile.
8. A new broom sweeps clean.
9. A prophet is not without honor save in his own country.
10. A rolling stone gathers no moss.
11. A stitch in time saves nine.
12. A thing of beauty is a joy forever.
13. All is fair in love and war.
14. All is not gold that glitters.
15. All's well that ends well.
16. All work and no play makes Jack a dull boy.
17. As the twig is bent, the tree is inclined.

18. Better late than never.
19. Birds of a feather flock together.
20. Children should be seen and not heard.
21. Christmas comes but once a year.
22. Coming events cast their shadows before.
23. Don't count your chickens before they are hatched.
24. Enough is as good as a feast.
25. Fine feathers make fine birds.
26. Give him an inch and he'll take an ell.
27. God helps those who help themselves.
28. Half a loaf is better than no bread.
29. Handsome is as handsome does.
30. He laughs best who laughs last.
31. Hitch your wagon to a star.
32. Honesty is the best policy.
33. If at first you don't succeed, try, try again.
34. In fair weather prepare for foul.
35. It is an ill wind that blows nobody good.
36. It is a long lane that has no turning.
37. Least said, soonest mended.
38. Listeners hear no good of themselves.
39. Love is blind.

40. Love laughs at locksmiths.
41. Make hay while the sun shines.
42. Money makes the mare go.
43. More haste, less speed.
44. Never leave till tomorrow that which you can do today.
45. No cross, no crown.
46. Nothing venture, nothing have.
47. One good turn deserves another.
48. Out of the frying pan into the fire.
49. Paddle your own canoe.
50. People who live in glass houses shouldn't throw stones.
51. Practise makes perfect.
52. Pride goeth before a fall.
53. Procrastination is the thief of time.
54. Sauce for the goose is sauce for the gander.
55. Slow but sure.
56. Spare the rod and spoil the child.
57. Sow the wind and reap the whirlwind.
58. The early bird catches the worm.
59. The eyes serve for ears to the deaf.
60. The last straw broke the camel's back.
61. The proof of a pudding is in the eating.

62. The reward of perseverance is sure.
63. The worm will turn.
64. There's many a slip 'twixt the cup and the lip.
65. Time and tide wait for no man.
66. Time is money.
67. Well begun is half done.
68. What can't be cured must be endured.
69. When poverty comes in at the door, love flies out at the window.
70. When the cat is away the mice will play.
71. Where there's a will, there's a way.
72. Where there's smoke, there's fire.
73. While there's life, there's hope.
74. You may lead a horse to water, but you cannot make him drink.
75. Zeal without knowledge is the sister of folly.

Colloquial Forms

241. The forms that are given below for practise are especially common in the asking of questions. The first few words of a question are frequently the key to the whole. To lose them means failure; to get them means success. The value of the repeated practise of these forms, thus fixing them in the visual memory, is therefore apparent.

The practise should be both with an assistant and with the mirror. As an example for the practise with an assistant, take the form, "How long." The assistant should compose sentences beginning with the form, and following it with each of the auxiliary verbs and any other words that commonly do follow it. Two or three sentences for each auxiliary verb should be given; these sentences should be varied in thought, and such as would be apt to be used with the form. Complete examples are here given for the form, "How long."

(1) How long have you been here?
    "   "   " they been abroad?
    "   "   " we been away from home?
    "   " has he been working?
    "   "   " he been out of work?
    "   "   " it been raining?
    "   " had the storm lasted?
    "   "   " they been out of town?

How long had you waited for me?
"   "   am I to wait for you?
"   "   "   I to practise my lesson?
"   "   is   the pencil?
"   "   "   the room?
"   "   "   the table?
"   "   are   you going to be in town?
"   "   "   you to be on the ocean?
"   "   "   they to remain West?
"   "   was the concert?
"   "   "   the opera?
"   "   "   the play?
"   "   were they in the city?
"   "   "   you on your vacation?
"   "   "   they to be abroad this
                                         summer?
"   "   will you be away?
"   "   "   they be in town?
"   "   "   he keep the secret?
"   "   would   you   be   willing   to
                                         wait?
"   "   "   you like to live abroad?
"   "   "   you like to live?
"   "   shall we put up with it?
"   "   "   I boil the eggs?
"   "   should we wait for him?
"   "   "   I chew my food?

How long do you think it will rain?
"   "   " they want to think the
                        matter over?
"   "   " we stop at Buffalo?
"   " does he expect to be gone?
"   "   " he stay abroad?
"   "   " the rainy season last?
"   " did they remain South?
"   "   " the storm last?
"   "   " you wait for me?
"   " may we use the 'phone?
"   "   " I keep the book?
"   "   " we have for study?
"   " might I have to walk?
"   "   " we have to wait?
"   " can you keep a secret?
"   "   " you hold your breath?
"   "   " you swim?
"   " could you keep quiet?
"   "   " they walk without stop-
                        ping?
"   " must we stay here?
"   "   " I practise my lesson?
"   " ought we to rest?
"   "   " she to remain South?
"   " before you will come back?
"   "   " she goes away?

How long ago were you in Washington?
"   "   "   were you abroad?
"   "   since you left New York?
"   "   "   you saw your friend?

In practising these forms before the mirror
the aim should be to familiarize the eye both
with the form and with the auxiliary verb
that follows it. Saying the complete sentence,
concentrate (but do not emphasize) on the
form "How long"; then repeat the sentence
and concentrate on the auxiliary verb. The
order of these verbs should be rearranged,
bringing together for contrast and comparison
those verbs that are apt to be confused. The
sentences do not need to be varied save as the
requirements of grammar may demand. The
sentences given below will illustrate these
points; the grouping of the verbs apt to be confused is indicated by the separating spaces. Go
over each group many times.

How long has he been here?
"   "   does "   stay   "   ?
"   "   is   "   to be   "   ?

"   "   has he been here ?
"   "   had "   "   "   ?
"   "   can "   be   "   ?

How long did he stay here?
"   "   is   " to be " ?

"   "   am I to be here?
"   "   may   he "   " ?
"   "   might "   "   " ?
"   "   must   "   "   " ?

"   "   was he to be here?
"   "   were you " "   " ?
"   "   will   " be   " ?
"   "   would   "   " ?

"   "   would you stay here?
"   "   could "   "   " ?
"   "   do   "   "   " ?

"   "   shall I be here?
"   "   should " "   " ?

"   "   have you been here?
"   "   are   " to be " ?
"   "   ought "   "   " ?

It is well, also, after having used the mirror, to practise the sentences according to this grouping with your assistant.

The methods of practise indicated for "How long" will apply also to the other forms which are here tabulated for convenience of use.

(2) How much have you left? . . .
    "   "   has . . . .
    "   "   had . . . .
    "   "   am . . . .
    "   "   is . . . .
    "   "   are . . . .
    "   "   was . . . . . .
    "   "   were . . . . . .
    "   "   will . . . . . .
    "   "   would . . . . . .
    "   "   shall . . . . . .
    "   "   should . . . . . .
    "   "   do . . . .
    "   "   does . . . . . .
    "   "   did . . . .
    "   "   may . . . . . .
    "   "   might . . . . . .
    "   "   can . . . . . .
    "   "   could . . . . . .
    "   "   must . . . . . .
    "   "   ought . . . . . .
    "   "   time have you left?

How much money will it take?
"   "   better this will be.
"   "   worse it might have been.

(3) How far have we come?
    "   "   has . . . .
    (etc., using all auxiliary verbs).

How far away is the river?
"   "   up the street is the house?
"   "   down shall I go?
"   "   back shall I sit?
"   "   ahead can you see?
"   "   front is your seat?

(4) How many have you told about it?
    "   "   has . . . .
    (etc., using all auxiliary verbs)

How many people were there?
"   "   mistakes have I made?
"   "   miles an hour can you walk?

(5) How soon have you planned to come?
    "   "   has . . . .
    (etc., using all auxiliary verbs)

(6) How hard have you tried?
    "   " has . . . .
    (etc., using all auxiliary verbs)
How hard it rains!
    "   " the wind blows!

At this point you should review exercises 1 to 6 inclusive, skipping around from one group to the other. For example:

> *How long* has he been here?
> *How hard* will he work?
> *How many* have been invited?
> *How far* may I walk with you?
> *How soon* am I to see you? etc.

(7) What have you done for him?
    " has . . . .
    (etc., using all auxiliary verbs)

(8) Why have . . . .
    (etc., using all auxiliary verbs)

(9) When have . . . . . .
    (etc., using all auxiliary verbs)

(10) Where have . . . . . .
    (etc., using all auxiliary verbs)

(11) Which have . . . . . .
    (etc., using all auxiliary verbs)

Which book do you want?
  " house do you like best?
  " way shall I go?
  " direction shall I take?
  " car do I take?
  " day suits you best?
  " hour do you prefer?

(12) Who or whom have . . . . .
  (etc., using all auxiliary verbs)

Exercises 7 to 12 inclusive should be reviewed in the same manner as exercises 1 to 6.

(13) Have I (we, you, they) . . . .
  Has he (she, it) . . . .
  Had I (he, she, it, we, you, they)
  (etc., using all auxiliary verbs and all pronouns).

(14)

Haven't . . .	Shouldn't . . .
Hasn't . . .	Don't . . . .
Hadn't . . .	Doesn't . . .
Isn't	Didn't. . . .
Aren't . . .	Mayn't . . .
Wasn't . . .	Mightn't . . .
Weren't . . .	Can't . . . .
Won't	Couldn't . . .
Wouldn't . . .	Mustn't . . .
Shan't . . .	Oughtn't . . .

Contrast Exercises (13) and (14) for review.

(15) Why haven't . . . .
　"　hasn't . . . .
　　(etc., using all negative contrac-
　　tions)

(16) I'm . . . .
　I'll . . . .
　I'd . . . .
　I've . . . .
　He's . . . .
　He'll . . . .
　He'd . . . .
　She's . . . .
　She'll . . . .
　She'd . . . .
　We're . . . .
　We'll . . . .
　We'd . . . .
　We've . . . .
　You're . . . .
　You'll . . . .
　You'd . . . .
　You've . . . .
　They're . . . .
　They'll . . . .
　They'd . . . .
　They've . . . .

SECTION VI

242. THE fact that the sounds in several consonant groups have the same visible movements gives rise to a considerable body of homophenous words—that is, words that look very similar or alike. The two sounds *f* and *v* in "few" and "view" appear exactly the same when the words are spoken naturally. So also do *p*, *b*, and *m* in the words "pie," "buy," and "my." Such words cannot be told apart by their formation unless the movements be exaggerated; and exaggeration, as has been said repeatedly, is something which the student must guard against most carefully lest false impressions be made and the eye be taught to expect facial characteristics which will never be seen in ordinary conversation. These words must be distinguished, then, not by their formation, but by the thought or context in which they are used.

The problem is similar to that which confronts those who are not deaf when called on to distinguish between such homophonous or like-sounding words as "seem" and "seam," "teem" and "team," "rough" and "ruff"; but the homophenous words far outnumber the homophonous, and by just so much is our problem more difficult of solution. And yet it is not so serious as it may seem at first sight. Take the two words "few" and "view"—it is hard to conceive of a sentence in which, if the rest of the sentence be understood, one of these words could be mistaken for the other. Surely it is easy enough to substitute the right word in "There is a beautiful —— from my window," or in, "I have only a —— minutes to spare." Or take the homophenous group, "pie," "buy," and "my,"—if at the table you should be asked: "Will you have a piece of apple ——?" I think you would answer "yes" without any qualms that you might be eating "buy" or "my." Our common sense solves this problem for us so frequently and so readily that the seriousness of it is much less than anyone without the experience would suppose.

In part the method of solving the problem

arising from homophenous words is by such work as I directed in Chapter V on the practise with stories—that is, practise in training the mind to grasp the thought as a whole. More particularly, however, the method should be devoted to exercises with homophenous words themselves. Notice first the origin of such words. The three sounds, *p*, *b*, and *m*, looking just alike, may be substituted one for the other in so far as the substitution permits forming another word. In the word "boom," substitute *p* for *b*, and also *p* for *m*, and you have "poop." But no other substitutions are possible here, for if we try to make them we get "poom," "poob," "boop," "moom, "moop," and "moob," none of which are words. Now, remembering again that *t*, *d*, and *n* all have the same movement, the flat-tongue-to-gum, see how many substitutions can be made in the word "bad" so as to create new words all of which are homophenous. Bad, bat, ban, band, pad, pat, pan, pant, mad, mat, man.

The sounds which have homophenous formations are, in the consonants, (1) *p*, *b*, *m;* (2) *f*, *v;* (3) *wh*, *w;* (4) *s*, *z*, soft *c;* (5) *sh*, *zh*, *ch*, *j*, (soft *g*); (6) *t*, *d*, *n;* (7) *k*, *g*, *ng*, *ck* and hard *c*.

The last two of these groups are also almost mutually homophenous. In the vowels we have no absolutely homophenous sounds, though short *ĕ* and long *ā* are so nearly alike as to be exceedingly difficult to distinguish except by the context of the sentence.

The list of homophenous words given below does not by any means exhaust the possibilities, but it is a fairly complete list of homophenes in common use. I arrange them according to the number of words in the group, first where there are two words that look alike, then three, and so on. For one lesson or practise period, about twenty to twenty-five words may be used. That is ten to twelve groups of two words each, seven or eight of three words, five or six of four words, four or five of five words, etc.

First, the student should memorize the words of each group selected for practise—that is, he should know each and all of the words of each homophenous group so that he can say them without referring to the printed page. Try the words also before the mirror to familiarize yourself with their formation.

Then compose sentences in your own mind for each of the words, as many sentences as are naturally suggested by them. The sentences should be simple, not involved, and the aim should be to compose the sentences quickly, not to stop and try to puzzle them out.

Finally, have your assistant compose for you sentences for each of the words. Preferably he should write the sentences down, and then read them to you; though if your assistant be apt at composing the sentences they may be given to you offhand. In any case they should be given smoothly and without hesitation. I find it advisable in changing from one group to another to tell the pupil only one of the words in the new group, and then give the sentences skipping around—that is, not in the order as the words stand.

I will give as examples sentences for a few of the groups given below:

Abuse, Amuse.—You should not abuse your privileges. Please amuse the baby for an hour.

Ascend, ascent, assent.—Will you ascend the mountain? I gave my assent to the plan. The ascent of the mountain is very rough. Will you ascend the rough ascent of the mountain? Will you give your assent for me to ascend the rough ascent of the mountain?

Air, hair, hare, heir.—Do you feel the air from the window? Did you ever hear of the race between the hare and the tortoise? She has beautiful long hair. She was heir to a large fortune.

If at any time you fail to understand the sentence, your assistant should write down for you some key word other than that one of the homophenous group that is being used. In the sentence, "She was heir to a large fortune," the word written for you should be "fortune," not "heir." Then try the sentence again.

The fewer the words in a group, the easier as a rule will the sentences be; so that the arrangement below gives the groups in the order of difficulty.

(1) Two words in a group:
abuse, amuse
allowed, aloud
bloom, plume
chair, share
chamois, shabby
choir, quire
class, glass
council, counsel
crease, grease

dazzle, tassel
displace, displays
draft, draught
falls, false
fault, vault
ferry, very
fogs, fox
grand, grant
guessed, guest
handsome, hansom
home, hope
lessen, lesson
liar, lyre
myth, pith
nerve, turf
omen, open
one, won
phonograph, photograph
profit, prophet
rough, ruff
shame, shape
sin, sit
smell, spell
smoke, spoke
smudge, sponge
suite, sweet
thawed, thought
yoke, yolk

(2) Three words in a group
abound, about, amount
act, hacked, hanged
ascend, ascent, assent
aught, awed, ought
beach, beech, peach
bird, burn, pert
blush, plunge, plush
chain, jade, shăde
clam, clamp, clap
chop, job, shop
cold, colt, gold
crack, crag, crank
croup, groom, group
dime, time, type
ear, hear, here
elm, helm, help
float, flowed, flown
foul, fowl, vowel
hoes, hose, owes
honor, otter, odder
idle, idol, idyl
jiggle, jingle, shingle
lack, lag, lank
luck, lug, lung
meal, peal, peel
plum, plumb, plump

rabbit, rabid, rapid
ran, rant, rat
ram, rap, wrap
roam, robe, rope
run, runt, rut
search, serge, surge
shone, showed, shown
slab, slam, slap
sleight, slide, slight
snare, stair, stare
snub, stub, stump
some, sum, sup
swab, swamp, swap
thick, thing, think
throat, throne, thrown
tread, dread, trend
which, wish, witch

(3) Four words in a group:
aid, ate, eight, hate
air, hair, hare, heir
all, awl, hall, haul
barge, march, marsh, parch
battle, paddle, mantel, mantle
beak, meek, peak, peek
birch, merge, purge, perch
black, blank, plank, plaque

bump, mum, pump, pup
cab, camp, cap, gap
choose, chews, juice, shoes
come, cub, cup, gum
creed, greed, green, greet
crutch, crunch, crush, grudge
colonel, kernel, curdle, girdle
dale, nail, tail, tale
dame, name, tame, tape
deep, deem, team, teem
die, dye, tie, nigh
doubt, down, town, noun
gild, gilt, guilt, killed
ground, crowd, crown, crowned
him, hip, hymn, imp
hinge, hitch, inch, itch
money, muddy, putty, bunny
raise, race, rays, raze
rank, rack, rag, rang
sack, sag, sang, sank
scene, seat, seed, seen
spine, smite, spied, spite
stud, stun, stunt, stunned
straight, strained, strait, strayed
truck, drug, drunk, trunk
wad, wan, wand, what
wait, wade, wane, weight

(4) Five words in a group:

beer, bier, mere, peer, pier
bob, mob, mop, pop, bomb
braid, brain, brayed, prate, prayed
bustle, muscle, mussel, muzzle, puzzle
chewed, chute, June, jute, shoot
crab, cram, cramp, grab, gramme
dim, dip, tip, nip, nib
dose, doze, toes, nose, knows
duck, dug, tongue, tuck, tug
earn, heard, herd, hurt, urn
guide, guyed, kind, kine, kite
hues, hews, ewes, yews, use
led, lead, lend, lent, let
missile, missal, mistle, pistil, pistol
neat, knead, need, dean, deed
plant, bland, plaid, plan, plat
rig, rick, ring, rink, wring
right, ride, rind, rite, write
shun, jut, shunt, shut, shunned
staid, stayed, stained, state
whig, wick, wig, wing, wink
white, whine, wide, wind, wine

(5) Six words in a group:

add, at, had, hand, hat, ant
badge, batch, match, patch, mash

back, bag, bang, bank, pack, pang

banner, banter, batter, manner, matter, patter

bare, bear, mare, pair, pare, pear

bud, but, bun, butt, mud, pun

can, canned, cant, can't, cad, cat

cent, scent, sent, send, said, set

coat, code, cone, cote, goad, goat

crate, crane, grade, grain, grate, great

done, dun, ton, none, nun, nut

fad, fan, fat, van, vat, fanned

knot, nod, not, dot, tot, don

raid, rain, rained, rate, reign, reigned

road, roan, rode, rote, rowed, wrote

(6) Seven words, in a group:

bold, bolt, mold, molt, poled, bowled,
polled

oound, bout, bowed, mound, mount,
pound, pout

brick, brig, bring, brink, prick, prig,
prink

dab, dam, damp, nap, nab, tab, tap

side, cite, sighed, sight, sign, signed,
site

wed, wen, wend, went, wet, when, whet

(7) Eight words in a group:

been, bin, pin, bit, bid, pit, pinned, mitt

dead, debt, den, dent, net, ten, tend, tent

don't, dote, tone, toned, towed, toad, note, known

medal, meddle, mettle, metal, pedal, peddle, petal, mental

(8) Nine words in a group:

bead, bean, beat, beet, mean, meat, meet, peat, mien

baize, base, bass, bays, mace, maize, maze, pace, pays

dew, due, do, to, too, two, new, knew, knu

buck, bug, bunk, muck, pug, bung, monk, mug, punk

(9) Ten words in a group:

bend, bent, mend, meant, penned, pent, bed, pen, bet, pet

boat, bone, bode, mode, moan, mote, moat, mowed, mown, moaned

died, dine, dyed, tide, tied, tight, tine, night, knight, nine

(10) Twelve words in a group:

bite, bide, mite, might, pied, bind, mind, pint, pine, pined, mine, mind

fade, fane, fate, feint, vain, faint, feign, feigned, fete, vane, vein, veined

(11) Fourteen words in a group:

bad, mad, pad, bat, mat, pat, ban, pan, pant, man, banned, panned, band, manned

bait, bane, bayed, made, maid, main, mate, mane, paid, pate, pane, pain, paint, pained

Enough material is given above to keep the student occupied for some time. Do not, however, devote all your time for practise in one day to this, or to any other one thing. Remember that it is the varied, all-around practise that develops the best lip-reader. After the homophenous words given have been completed, go through them again in review.

In addition it will be found helpful to do original work in thinking out groups of homophenous words for yourself. Given one word, try to find all possible homophenes;

and when you have found them, practise as previously directed. I give herewith a few words which will serve as a basis for this work, but when this list is exhausted, select other words yourself from any source:

(12) whom	creep	chord	baggage
beam	dry	malt	brace
prove	eve	fur	firm
brim	whip	pew	five
buy	ripe	birth	leaf
love	owl	flower	pull
poor	light	fight	warm
pod	spear	hiss	strive
muss	jam	push	tell
friend	aim	fair	comb

A still further source of material may be found in my pamphlet "The Use of Homophenous Words," published by The Volta Bureau, Washington, D. C.

APPENDICES

APPENDIX A
TABLE OF VOWELS AND DIPHTHONGS

Accented Vowels	Example	Movements
long ā	face	extended-medium + relaxed-narrow
short ă	mat	extended-wide
Italian a (ah)	far	relaxed-wide
broad a (aw)	awe	puckered-wide
â before strong r	tare	extended-medium
long ē	be	extended-narrow
short ĕ	get	extended-medium
ē before strong r	fierce	relaxed-narrow
long ī	giant	relaxed-wide + relaxed-narrow
short ĭ	pit	relaxed-narrow
long ō	ope	puckered-wide + puckered-variable
short ŏ	con, off	relaxed-wide, or puckered-wide
ō before strong r	ore	puckered-wide
long ōō	too	puckered-narrow
short ŏŏ	full	puckered-medium
ōō before strong r	sure	puckered-medium
ow, ou	how, out	relaxed-wide + puckered-variable
oy	boy	puckered-wide + relaxed-narrow
long ū	accuse	relaxed-narrow + puckered-narrow
short ŭ	up	relaxed-medium
ū before r	cure	relaxed-narrow + puckered-medium

318

Unaccented Vowels	Example	Movements
long ā	surface	relaxed-narrow, or relaxed-medium
short ă	material	relaxed-medium
Italian a (ah)	sofa	relaxed-medium
broad a (aw)	august (adj.)	puckered-wide, or relaxed-medium
â before strong r	elementary	relaxed-narrow, or relaxed-medium
long ĕ	befall	relaxed-narrow, or relaxed-medium
short ĕ	target	relaxed-narrow, or relaxed-medium
ĕ before strong r	ferocious	relaxed-narrow, or relaxed-medium
long ī	gigantic	relaxed-narrow, or relaxed-medium
short ĭ	pulpit	relaxed-narrow, or relaxed-medium
long ŏ	opinion	relaxed-medium
short ŏ	convince, official	relaxed-medium
ŏ before strong r	oration	relaxed-medium
long o͞o	today	puckered-medium, or relaxed-medium
short o͞o	awful	relaxed-medium
oo before strong r	erasure	relaxed-medium
long ū	accusation	rel.-nar.+puck.-med., or rel-nar+rel.-med.
short ŭ	upon	relaxed-medium
ū before r	accurate	relaxed-narrow + relaxed-medium

APPENDIX B

TABLE OF CONSONANTS

The consonants are here arranged alphabetically for convenience of reference.

b, as in "bat," lip-shut
c (soft) as in "cent," tremor-at-corners
c (hard), as in "cat," throat movement
ch (soft), as in "church," lip-projected
ch (hard), as in "choir," throat movement
d, as in "die," flat-tongue-to-gum
f, as in "few," lip-to-teeth
g (soft), as in "gem," lip-projected
g (hard), as in "go," throat movement
h, as in "he," no movement
j, as in "jam," lip-projected
k, as in "kin," throat movement
l, as in "leaf," pointed-tongue-to-gum
m, as in "my," lip-shut
n, as in "nigh," flat-tongue-to-gum
ng, as in "rang," throat movement
nk, as in "rank," throat movement
p, as in "pie," lip-shut
ph, as in "sylph," lip-to-teeth
q, as in "quart," throat movement
r, as in "reef," puckered-corners
s, as in "saw," tremor-at-corners

sh, as in "ship," lip-projected
t, as in "tie," flat-tongue-to-gum
th, as in "thigh," and "thy," tongue-to-teeth
v, as in "view," lip-to-teeth
w, as in "war," puckered-variable
wh, as in "wharf," puckered-variable
x, as in "box," throat movement+tremor-at-corners
x, as in "Xenia," tremor-at-corners
y, as in "you," relaxed-narrow
z, as in "zone," tremor-at-corners
z (zh), as in "azure," lip-projected

APPENDIX C

BIBLIOGRAPHY OF BOOKS ON LIP-READING

INSTRUCTION BOOKS

BÉLANGER (Adolphe), La Lecture sur les Lévres; Atelier Typographique de l'Institution Nationale des Sourds-Muets, Paris.

BELL (Alexander Melville), Facial Speech Reading and Articulation Teaching; Volta Bureau, Washington, D. C.

BOUDIN (Étienne), La Surdité: Moyen d'y Remédier par la Lecture sur les Levres; A. Maloine, Paris.

BOULTBEE (E. F.), Practical Lip-Reading; L. U. Gill, London.

COUPLIN (Mary), How to Understand Without Sound; W. H. Needham Co., Sigourney, Ia.

DREBUSCH (F.), Der Absehunterricht mit Schwerhörigen und Ertaubten; Berlin.

DROUOT (E.), La Lecture sur les Lévres; Chez l'Auteur, 19, rue Vauquélin, Paris.

GUTZMANN (Hermann), Facial Speech Reading; Volta Bureau, Washington, D. C.

HARTMANN (Arthur), Lehr-und Lernbuch für Schwerhörige zur Erlernung des Absehens vom Munde; J. F. Bergmann, Wiesbaden.

HEWETT (E. K.), Lip-Reading for the Deaf; The Harewood Press. London.

MÜLLEK (Julius), Das Absehen der Schwerhörigen; Johannes Kriebel, Hamburg.

NITCHIE (Edward B.), Self-Instructor in Lip-Reading; Lessons in Lip-Reading for Self-Instruction; Lip-Reading Simplified; Lessons in Lip-Reading, Revised Edition, and accompanying Teachers' Handbook; Surdus Publishing Company, New York.

PARSONS (Mary Hepburn), The Reading of Speech from the Lips; Akerman Company, Providence, R. I.

RÖTZER (Franz Xaver), Ubungsbuch für Schwerhörige und Ertaubte Das Ablesen vom Munde; R. Oldenbourg, München and Berlin.

SNOW (Emma), My List of Homophenous Words; Volta Bureau, Washington, D. C.

STORY (A. J.), Speech-Reading; Yellon, Williams & Co., Ltd., London.

WOLLERMANN (Rudolf, Otto, und Emil), Lehr-und Lernbuch für den Absehunterricht; Teetzmann & Randel, Stettin.

HISTORICAL OR SUGGESTIVE

Report of Fourth Summer Meeting of the A. A. P. T. S. D.,—the following addresses: Experiences in Lip-Reading, S. G. Davidson; Experiences of a Speech-Reader, Mrs. Sylvia C. Balis; "Further Contribution to the study of that Subtile Art which may Inable one with an Observant Eie to Heare what any Man Speaks by the Moving of the Lips," Mrs. Alexander Graham Bell; The Teaching of Speech-Reading to Adults, Sarah Allen Jordan; Speech-Reading, Susan E. Bliss; Speech-Reading, Mabel Ellery Adams; Volta Bureau, Washington, D. C.

JONES (Mary Davis), Some Suggestions about Lip-Reading; Volta Bureau, Washington, D. C.

KENNEDY (Mildred), Mirror Practise as an Aid to Lip-Reading; Volta Bureau, Washington, D. C.

BOOKS ON ALLIED SUBJECTS

BELL (Alexander Graham), The Mechanism of Speech; Funk & Wagnalls Company, New York.

BELL (Alexander Melville), Sounds and Their Relations, and also other works on Visible Speech; Volta Bureau, Washington, D. C.

CARRUTHERS (S. W.), A Contribution to the Mechanism of Articulate Speech; The Edinburgh Medical Journal, Edinburgh.

WAY (Daisy M.), The Whipple Natural Alphabet; Volta Bureau, Washington, D. C.

Printed in the United States
90990LV00003B/203/A